Mayfi  rv

D0438527

BIOETHICS AND THE NEW
MEDICAL TECHNOLOGY

BIOETHICS & THE NEW MEDICAL TECHNOLOGY

MARGOT C. J. MABIE

ATHENEUM 1993
New York

MAXWELL MACMILLAN CANADA
Toronto

MAXWELL MACMILLAN INTERNATIONAL
New York Oxford Singapore Sydney

ATHENEUM
Macmillan Publishing Company
866 Third Avenue
New York, NY 10022

MAXWELL MACMILLAN CANADA, INC.
1200 Eglinton Avenue East
Suite 200
Don Mills, Ontario M3C 3N1

Macmillan Publishing Company is part of the Maxwell Communication
Group of Companies.

Book design by Crowded House Design

First edition

Printed in the United States of America
10 9 8 7 6 5 4 3 2 1

Library of Congress Cataloging-in-Publication Data
Mabie, Margot C. J.
Bioethics and the new medical technology / Margot C. J. Mabie.—1st ed.
        p.   cm.
Includes bibliographical references and index.
Summary: Examines some of the ethical questions raised by the
capabilities of modern medicine.
ISBN 0-689-31637-2
1. Medical ethics—Juvenile literature.   2. Bioethics—Juvenile
literature.   3. Human reproductive technology—Moral and ethical
aspects—Juvenile literature.   4. Genetic engineering—Moral and ethical
aspects—Juvenile literature.   [1. Bioethics.]   I. Title.
R724.M155   1993
174'.2—dc20   92-22642

For my mother,
Nancy Parsons Jones

CONTENTS

Preface	xi
The Principles	1
Understanding Ourselves	21
Bioethics at the End of Life	47
Bioethics at the Beginning of Life	73
Bioethics and Costs	93
Personal Rules, Society's Rules	117
Notes	141
Glossary	149
Suggested Reading	153
Acknowledgments	157
Index	159

*It has been said that ethics like art is
precisely a matter of knowing where to draw lines.*

—DANIEL MAGUIRE

PREFACE

Accustomed as we are to thinking of medicine as a science, it is hard to keep in mind that before World War II, the profession was more of an art. Then, physicians had only a rudimentary understanding of the human body and a paltry collection of methods by which to address disease. Their role was first and foremost to provide care and comfort. Neither they nor their patients had great expectations for cure. Today physicians have a vastly enlarged comprehension of the body's workings and an astonishing technology—the entire array of tools and machinery; laboratory, medical, and surgical procedures; and drugs. With those, they have prolonged, enhanced, saved—some would say, even created—lives.

Impressive as medicine already is, the limits of the field seem nowhere in sight. Indeed, researchers are barely at the threshold of many areas of inquiry. Gains are made at an ever quicker pace. The sophisticated information, equipment, techniques, and drugs that bedazzle us now will no doubt seem crude in twenty years' time.

But the technology that has proved so helpful for so many brings with it a burden that we are only beginning to acknowledge. Medicine as an art rested on venerable assumptions that frequently prove inadequate for the questions posed by medicine as a science—biomedicine. The air of urgency in answering these questions arises because medicine today is pressing hard and insistently at the edges of life itself. What is life? When does it begin, and when does it end? What are our responsibilities to life? Despite its intent, does modern medicine's wizardry occasionally drive us to devalue life?

The myriad new medical technologies demand that we consider far more than the medical effectiveness of a particular procedure. At the beginning of life, the new reproductive technologies call into question our traditional concept of the family and how it is created. Prenatal testing, which can detect many genetic and developmental problems in the unborn, may lead to an increase in the age-old practice of abortion. Gene therapy, by which we might intervene to reformulate the genetic makeup of future generations, is on the horizon. With the ability to foresee or fiddle with various human traits comes the worry that we will grow more intolerant of imperfection, an inherent aspect of human life.

A brier patch of problems grows at the other end of life, too. With the new technology, dying can often be a long, drawn-out process. Ventilators, feeding tubes, the various blinking and whirring machines, subtle chemical evaluations, and powerful, specific drugs—all have given many safe passage through hitherto deadly straits. But they have also sustained many in a limbo that is arguably not life and unarguably not quality life. Out of this have come justifications for euthanasia—active and passive, voluntary and involuntary—and for suicide, even assisted suicide.

Between the ends of life are other bedeviling issues. For

example, the new medical technology has made organ transplantation almost mundane, but the scarcity of organs requires stark decisions about which patients will get first crack at the precious few that come available. Scarcity threatens not just those people who anxiously await, in a kind of psychological suspended animation, an organ for transplantation. Our society, reeling from the cost of what we already have, may have to postpone or forgo developing some promising technologies simply because they are too expensive. The high cost of health care pinches our purse, for we have less to spend on all the other things that we need or want in order to make life meaningful. It pinches our conscience, too, for many Americans are denied even the most basic health care because they cannot afford *any* health care.

Ethics is the area of philosophy that considers human conduct. Bioethics focuses specifically on how the gleanings of the biological sciences are to be applied to the practice of medicine. Scientific knowledge is in itself amoral. It is how we get and use scientific knowledge that is moral or immoral. Bioethics uses an interdisciplinary approach: philosophers, theologians, historians, writers, lawyers, as well as scientists— all contribute their distinctive perceptions in a group effort to define the problems and find their solutions. Yet bioethics is not merely an academic field. It falls to all of us to understand the issues and frame a bioethical system for ourselves, both as individuals and as a society. Each of us will be called upon to make personal bioethical decisions at one time or another. And the bioethical positions we codify in law or regulation, binding on all of us, will both reflect and shape all of the values by which our society coheres.

THE PRINCIPLES

One feature that distinguishes human beings from all other creatures is the need to philosophize. The drive to account for one's life—to understand the forces that gave rise to it, the meaning that can derive from it—begs for satisfaction. Everyone addresses that drive in his or her own way. Some find in religion a full and compelling account of life and how it should be lived. Others, for whom religion has less or no meaning, take a stringently rational approach. Using their capacity to reason, another distinctively human feature, they analyze their world to isolate principles and devise a philosophical system that can be every bit as elaborate as any religion. Still others find philosophical systems based on either religion or reason to be overly intellectual. Instead they rely on what might be called emotional antennae, feelings that suggest a consonance between the reality of the world and the reality of the self.

Regardless of the approach, what impels most of us to understand our life is a deep appreciation of its beauty and value. Those who are religious speak of the sanctity of life: life as God's most precious gift. Those who are not religious also speak of a reverence for life, for the very experience of life is a powerfully felt mystery. Ecstasies and sorrows, hopes fulfilled and hopes dashed, yearnings and contentment—all are part and parcel of the human experience. The instinct to hold on to life, even when we are assailed by suffering, is very strong.

We humans are also intensely social. Our lives are made up of a web of alliances with other humans, beginning with our parents. We gather in families, in communities, in societies, both for the closeness that can offer security and for the expansiveness that can unlock our finest selves. As children we depend on our parents to protect and sustain us physically and emotionally. As students we look to teachers to explain the workings of the world. As workers and parents we are potent agents of vitality. As friends we assuage our own and another's separateness—a fundamental fact of existence. Living our own lives, we at the same time add to and embroider others' lives and all of life with threads of a hue and texture uniquely our own.

The way we deal with others in large measure determines the extent and nature of our humanity. Ethics are principles of right conduct, and as such they concern those dealings. The alliances between humans are extraordinary in their complexity. There is an infinity of ways in which each of us can touch or be touched by others. Every human interaction, be it ordering a deli sandwich or rhapsodically falling in love, involves ethics. Some ethical decision making is dramatic. Taking a classic example, we can ponder the ethics of sacrificing some passengers so that others might survive in a lifeboat in danger of going down because it is overloaded. In our daily lives, however, most ethical decision making is not as stark. The supermarket checker, new to the job and flustered by a long line of impatient shoppers, has not rung up some of my purchases. What should I do? Day in, day out, we *live* ethics, rarely recognizing the fact that we refer to our own ethical system over and over again.

Our ethics are to a considerable extent a reflection of the society we live in, an outgrowth of our community's values, goals, and social arrangements. These can vary greatly. For example, Asian societies tend to put the community first, believing that a flourishing community makes for flourishing individuals. Americans, by contrast, tend to put the individual first, believing that by fostering individual development, the community's welfare is ensured. Such views account for differences in every facet of life.

Ethics can vary greatly within a single society, too. Fundamentalists who believe in a severe God and the inerrancy of the Bible have an outlook on what is acceptable and what is desirable that is very different from the views of those who believe in a loving God and the social gospel.

Ethics are nonetheless intensely personal. We first receive ethics from our parents and our society. Then, as we take charge of our lives, we modify those ethics to fit our own view of the world. Each of us has an ethical system that is as unique and distinctive as our fingerprint. Ethics are also attached to the innermost fibers of our being. Conscience, which can tweak or lash, is proof of that.

The philosopher Henry David Aiken lays out the way we determine what is good or right, what we ought to do, as a four-tiered process.[1] The first tier, which he calls the expressive-evocative level, is characterized by off-the-cuff reactions to a given situation. On hearing that someone dying a painful death has asked for euthanasia—that is, for someone to kill him or her to end the pain—we might say, "Oh, that's terrible!" The response is essentially emotional. We do not stop to sort out the reasons why it might be terrible.

At the next level, what Aiken calls the moral level, we are asked to square our view of what one ought to do in this particular situation. We explain our emotional response by citing a moral rule. "Killing is wrong," we might say.

We are forced to Aiken's third tier, the ethical level, when the moral rule that seems to apply for the case at hand does not feel right. Perhaps another moral rule conflicts, making just as strong a claim for a different action. We might, for example, say, "We are morally obligated to help people when we can provide what they need. If we have no narcotic that can provide the longed-for release from pain, are we not obligated to help by allowing for euthanasia?" Or perhaps following the moral rule will result only in making life rougher or more painful. When we refuse to allow euthanasia, we often prolong pain. Perhaps the moral rule, applied over and over again, has come to feel uncomfortable. More and more, there are cases of people driven to consider euthanasia. Perhaps changes in society have created a situation that the moral rule does not address. Medicine today can often sustain life in a ravaged body. But for all its powers, it cannot always quiet pain.

Whatever the reason for moving to the ethical level, the style of questioning changes. Questions must first be shucked of the specifics of the particular situation involving particular people. Individual cases invariably engender an urgency that can cloud our thinking. At the ethical level we set aside our personal moral rules and turn to ethical principles, the very general expressions of primary values from which moral rules derive. We might ask, "Does our prohibition against euthanasia truly support our belief in the value of life?" As Aiken notes, ethical principles are so broad and so abstract that the modification of one ethical principle can necessitate extensive renovations of one's entire moral rule system.

Aiken's fourth tier, what he calls the postethical, or human, level, is where the question "Why should I be moral?" is asked. Ethical principles and moral rules bind us to patterns of conduct only insofar as they are truly important to us. At this level we sign on or sign off. It is we who give ethics and morality their legitimacy and power.

Ethics as an area of philosophical inquiry had its first flowering in ancient Greece. Since then there have been advanced myriad ethical systems, each distinguished from the others by its particular view of what it means to be human. Most can be classified in one of two groups. Deontological theories are based on duty, either duty to God's will, duty to the laws of nature, duty to moral rules arrived at by common sense, or duty to the obligations that spring from a hypothetical social contract. Teleological theories, on the other hand, hold that the correctness of a moral decision is measured by the good that it produces. While deontologists debate what constitutes duty, teleologists debate what is good and how best to attain that good.

The dichotomy in deontological and teleological theories can be seen in the responses to the proposal that school systems provide condoms to their students. A deontologist might say that it is morally reprehensible to distribute condoms to teenagers. That only encourages relationships for which teenagers are emotionally unprepared. Further, with the specter of teen pregnancy and AIDS, such relationships can be destructive, even deadly. Agreeing that teenage sex is damaging in every regard, a teleologist might say that it is morally reprehensible not to distribute condoms. Many teenagers are sexually active despite efforts to inculcate the ideal of sex for married adults. Refusing to distribute condoms is stiff-necked adherence to a rule that will only result in misery. Distribution may result in decreasing the incidence of both pregnancy and AIDS—that is the greater good.

Professional ethics—principles that apply to the conduct of, say, lawyers or politicians—are developed by members of the profession, who pluck from general ethics those principles that are especially pertinent to their work. The Oath of Hippocrates was the first code of professional ethics for physicians. There is significant disagreement about whether Hippocrates, a fifth- and fourth-century B.C. physician who established a school for physicians on the Greek island of Kos, wrote any of the sixty to one hundred treatises that make up the Hippocratic Corpus, or even the oath itself. But the oath that bears his name remains the taproot of our Western society's medical ethics. Indeed, even today some medical school students take the oath upon graduation. Some of the oath is a sort of contractual agreement between student and teacher. For example, the student swears to instruct, without fee, the teacher's children if they, too, wish to learn the art of medicine. Some of it deals with the physician's obligations to the patient—for one, confidentiality. Other parts take up medical practice, favoring the use of dietetics for cure and forbidding abortion and assisted suicide. One point that the oath makes is critically important: The physician's job is to benefit the patient, and the physician is to do nothing that might be harmful. Even then there was a clear-eyed recognition that medicine itself has an extraordinary capacity to cause suffering as well as comfort.

The Hippocratic school of medicine was not at all in step with the medical practice of its day. At that time medicine was based on religious precepts and superstitions jumbled with observations on the workings of the human body. Physicians were actively involved in assisted suicide, abortion, and infanticide, all of which were common.

So for centuries the mainstream of the profession ignored the Hippocratic school, its oath and its precepts. Only with the rise of Christianity was there an institution that had an outlook consonant with the ideals of Hippocratic ethics. The concept of the physician's being called, which runs through the oath, has an analogue in Christianity, which urges its adherents to follow the call of God. Respect for the body and for life, along with the acceptance of medicine's limits implied by the pledge to do no harm, dovetailed neatly with the church's view that we are stewards of our bodies and our lives, God's greatest gift.

Mobilizing a sense of compassion, the church built and administered hospices where the ill, the orphaned, and travelers could come for care, and it served as the dominant force supporting, shaping, and formalizing the medical profession. The church also began developing a large and highly detailed body of literature on medicine and health in the context of Christian morality.

Beginning in the twelfth century, physicians were increasingly subject to regulation by secular law and, from within, by their newly developed guilds. To ensure high standards and to limit membership, the guilds paid close attention to the educational requirements for physicians, surgeons, and apothecaries. These professional organizations established fee schedules and codified professional ethics, which in the main pertained to the personal relationship between physician and patient and between physician and physician.

The principle of nonmaleficence—the obligation to do no harm—and the principle of beneficence—the duty to help—which appeared in the Oath of Hippocrates, are the first two principles undergirding the practice of medicine. Indeed, they were for more than two millennia the only principles on which the practice of medicine was based.

To illustrate the principle of nonmaleficence, many cite the case of Joseph Saikewicz. In 1976, at the age of sixty-seven, Saikewicz was found to have acute myeloblastic monocytic leukemia. The cancer was incurable; however, chemotherapy might hold the disease at bay. Virtually everyone with this form of cancer tried chemotherapy. In 30 to 50 percent of those cases—less for patients over the age of sixty—chemotherapy produced a remission for two to thirteen months. (Even today the prognosis for patients with this form of cancer is only slightly better.)

Whether Saikewicz was to have chemotherapy had to be determined by the courts. With an IQ of ten and a mental age of three years, he had been institutionalized since the age of thirteen and was unable to make the decision for himself. The court-appointed guardian *ad litem,* a person empowered to make medical decisions for someone who cannot, recommended no treatment. The chemotherapy is painful and often produces serious side effects. The benefit of possibly longer life was outweighed by the harm that treatment would cause: Saikewicz would have had to be tied down for treatment; the fright of treatment, the pain, and the wretched side effects would be crueler still because Saikewicz was unable to understand them. The probate court agreed, a decision that was upheld by the Supreme Judicial Court of Massachusetts. Saikewicz died peacefully two months later.[2]

Nonmaleficence is termed a negative duty because to do one's duty, one must do nothing. Beneficence, on the other hand, is a positive duty. Preventing harm, removing harm, doing good, however you slice it, beneficence requires that one *do* something. An example of beneficence is provided by the case of Alyssa Smith. Just twenty-one months old, she needed a new liver. At the time, such transplants required cadaveric livers—livers taken from the recently dead—and they are scarce. Further, liver transplants for children have not had a very good success rate. Using a new procedure, physicians thought they could take a lobe from Alyssa's mother's liver and transplant it to the toddler. Teresa Smith's remaining section of liver would be expected to grow back to its normal size, and the lobe transplanted to Alyssa would be expected to grow to full size, too.

The duty to beneficence can be limited if fulfilling it entails risk, and the risk to Alyssa's mother was seen as considerable. She would be subjected to surgery (a risk in its own right), the disturbance of her liver, and loss of her gall bladder, too. As a consequence Alyssa's physicians debated for a year whether the procedure should even be proposed to Alyssa's parents. Many believe that the mere existence of the option creates an impossible moral bind for a parent, demanding that he or she accept significant personal risks to help a dying child. But the procedure was proposed, and Alyssa's mother volunteered eagerly: "Once you've given someone a big piece of your heart, it's easy to throw in a little bit of liver," she quipped.[3]

That risk can limit one's duty to beneficence, at least from a legal standpoint, is demonstrated by the case of Robert McFall. Physicians who diagnosed his aplastic anemia gave him a 25 percent chance of surviving for a year. With a bone marrow transplant, they believed his chances of surviving for a year would increase to 40 to 60 percent. McFall's six brothers and sisters were found to be unsuitable as donors because of incompatibility. David Shimp, his cousin, proved a perfect match when tested for tissue compatibility, but he refused to undergo the second test, for genetic compatibility. Claiming that he worried about the risks of surgery and the ability of his marrow to regenerate, he would not under any circumstances be a donor for his cousin.

McFall went to court to compel Shimp to finish the testing and, if compatible, be a donor. McFall's lawyer argued—accurately—that taking marrow from a donor carries an extremely low risk and that marrow invariably replaces itself within days. The judge, while ruling that Shimp was under no legal obligation to donate marrow, described his refusal as "morally indefensible." Unlike Alyssa's mother, who overlooked real risk in her duty to beneficence, Shimp chose the opposite response. McFall died two weeks after the court ruling.[4]

Toward the end of the nineteenth century the reorientation of medicine as an art to medicine as a science began to take hold. Physicians committed themselves to harnessing science for the care, even cure, of their patients. Science, always a contributor to medical practice, would systematically be made its basis. Armed by science, physicians might increasingly gain control over the body's sometimes willful, unruly ways. So armed, physicians might prove more successful at prolonging life.

Building up the scientific basis for biomedicine took decades. Only around the time of World War II did the art really give way to the science. This shift, of immense importance in its own right, has precipitated other changes in the profession of medicine. To begin, the profusion of information and the pace at which that information is being expanded and refined has brought specialization. No physician can absorb all of the large body of information and blizzard of literature generated by medical research. Allowing the physician to concentrate on one area, specialization promotes more accurate and subtle diagnosis and treatment.

Specialization has also led to the concentration of medical care in large medical complexes, with correspondingly large staffs. Each member of the staff has narrowly defined tasks. All are organized to maximize efficiency. Biomedicine is very, very expensive, so expensive that society as a whole has been called upon to underwrite its development. We have spent lavishly on medical education, research, and all the technology by which medicine today is practiced. The best return on that investment requires full, streamlined utilization of professionals and technology.

Specialization and concentration, however, have some distinct drawbacks. Patients must cope with emotional and social, as well as physical, consequences of illness. Disfigurement; restrictions in diet, mobility, and personal expression; fear so gripping that it prevents meaningful communication with others—all these can be so isolating as to make the patient's sense of isolation a very real, very serious problem in its own right. This the specialist, focusing on only one organ, physiological system, or form of treatment, does not always see. Further, the specialist often is not equipped to deal with those consequences of illness precisely because they are emotional or social, not medical. Patients can feel similarly dehumanized in large medical complexes. They may encounter scores of staff members, but many of those encounters are brief and tightly focused.

The principles of beneficence and nonmaleficence, which sufficed as medicine's primary ethical guides well into the twentieth century, were found wanting as medicine moved into the burgeoning world of science and specialization. The consequent alterations in the health care system forced the addition of other guiding principles. The first to emerge was the principle of justice, which is seen most clearly in terms of individual rights.

The elaboration of individual rights began in earnest in the late seventeenth century. Sparked by the growing power and complexity of the state and the resulting tensions between the state and the individual, many philosophers of that time held that the individual has certain fundamental rights that cannot be abridged by the state. The state is said to be just only to the extent that it respects those rights. One forerunner of such rights theories was the ancient and medieval doctrine of natural law—the rules of nature or God that all humans, as creatures of nature or God, should live by. Another forerunner was the humanistic view, which emerged in the Renaissance. The individual then came to be seen as a rational creature with personal dignity and value that must be respected. The philosopher John Locke viewed life, liberty, and property as natural rights. Later, as philosophers expanded the thinking on rights, many came to regard the right to health as a logical outgrowth of the natural right to life. Thus the state must ensure its citizens' right to health care.

While Europeans accepted health care as a right, Americans ducked the issue. For a long time charity hospitals were able to meet the needs of those who could not afford health care. The principle of beneficence, hand in hand with an ideal of charity, kept those hospitals going. Rights were not a part of the calculus. That is no longer the case. As physicians began wielding technology to intervene and truly alter the course of disease, the increasing cost of care could no longer be met by charity. Government took on the problem. In 1965 Medicaid was set up to ensure that health care was available to all, regardless of the ability to pay. But federal and state moneys for Medicaid are limited. Skyrocketing costs have meant that more and more Americans—and not just the poor—go without. Strapped, we are only now getting down to deciding if the individual has a right to health care and, if so, just what justice requires that we provide.

The only feature common to all the many theories of justice is a maxim attributed to Aristotle: Equals should be treated equally, and unequals should be treated unequally. The first difficulty comes with the attempt to define the categories. What features make a group of individuals equals? How much difference among equals can there be before they become unequals, deserving separate classification? The second difficulty comes with the attempt to define what people deserve, what they are due. What constitutes proper treatment for each group? Determining what is required and what is optional is hotly debated. This is not a problem unique to medicine. Take, for example, education. Is a sports program essential to education, or is it a frill? Justice demands that the claims of unequals be satisfied, too, but they will not be satisfied in the same way. Consider the different sort of education mentally or physically handicapped students need.

Depending on one's philosophy, the principle of justice can be tightly constricted or broadly expansive. Libertarians hold that justice demands that the individual be free to pursue what he or she wants. Society can limit the individual's liberty only to the extent necessary to guarantee fair procedures. Egalitarians hold that there are inequalities that come of birth, natural abilities, and historical accident. The lucky have not earned all of their advantages, and justice permits some redistribution of society's benefits to the genuinely needy who are not responsible for their misfortune. Utilitarians accept social intervention to redistribute goods and wealth to the extent that that redistribution provides the most good to the largest number of people.

When justice cannot be satisfied completely because of a lack of resources, we are pressed to find a way to distribute those resources that are available. Here again there is wrangling about how to divide resources and how much is allotted to each. Do you simply give an equal share to each person, or do you determine share by individual need? To what extent do you adjust share to reflect the social contribution made by each person? Do you abandon these considerations and leave it to the marketplace to set how much each person receives? All these criteria for distributing resources are defensible. In fact, all are used, even within the same context. Consider education. Our public school system was established to give a basic education to each child. Special programs for children with, say, learning disabilities are built into the system for those students who need them. Scholarships are given to students who distinguish themselves as good citizens or good scholars. Parents with the financial wherewithal can elect to send their children to private schools.

One example of conflict over what the principle of justice requires by way of the provision of health care came up in 1988 when Varian Schmokel sued the state of Vermont. Eligible for Medicaid, Schmokel was scheduled for a liver transplant, but the state said that it would not pay for the surgery. Vermont's Medicaid regulations prohibited state funds for liver transplants for all patients over the age of eighteen. Schmokel sued, arguing that her right to equal protection under the law had been abridged. She was arguing, in effect, that her right to health, to life, was equal to that of, say, a seventeen-year-old and that health care resources were being unfairly distributed. The Vermont Superior Court agreed. But by then she was comatose. Two hours after the court ordered that the state pay for a transplant, she died.[5]

*   *   *

The fourth principle guiding medicine today is autonomy. The principle of autonomy respects each person as unique and irreplaceable, with the right to determine his or her own destiny. To try to control the individual is to run roughshod over personal dignity and to use him or her for one's own purposes.

Only in this century has autonomy become of real concern because only in this century have physicians had a significant ability to cure. Biomedicine has opened up the world of choice. Many diseases can be approached in many different ways. Consider cancer: surgery, radiation, and chemotherapy can be used, alone or in a variety of combinations. Autonomy is meaningful only in the context of choice.

Yet autonomy's ranking as a principle of medical ethics did not come in response to the right of the patient to choose among various courses of treatment. It came in response to revelations concerning experimentation. First and most powerful was the discovery at the Nuremberg Trials of the grisly experiments Nazi physicians had conducted on unwilling subjects. Later, in the 1960s and early 1970s, some questionable experiments conducted in the United States came to light. A few were blatantly abusive. At the Jewish Chronic Disease Hospital elderly patients were injected with live cancer cells. Mentally retarded children enrolled at Willowbrook State School were exposed to hepatitis for a study of that disease. Finally, it was learned that patients in the Tuskegee Syphilis Study, begun in 1932 to study the end stages of syphilis, were left to languish even after a cure for syphilis, penicillin, was found—this despite the fact that the end stages of syphilis were well understood.[6] Each episode was a distressing reminder that one could not dismiss Nazi experiments as a bizarre anomaly.

Hewing to the principle of autonomy means allowing

people to make decisions for themselves, even decisions that by all medical standards are considered unwise. Take, for example, the case of a Jehovah's Witness who gave birth to a daughter who, physicians asserted, needed a blood transfusion. Jehovah's Witnesses believe that it is a sin to accept blood products; accordingly, the parents refused to consent to transfusions for the infant. The hospital obtained a court order, and treatment was begun. At the same time, the mother began to hemorrhage, necessitating a hysterectomy. Her husband gave permission for surgery but not for transfusion. The judge, having ordered transfusions for the infant, declined to do the same for the mother, who died several hours later.[7]

Here the mother's autonomy, her right to determine treatment for herself, was respected. But the judge determined that her right to refuse transfusions does not extend to her infant. The state exercised its duty to protect the child, who had not had an opportunity to embrace or reject for herself her parents' religious views on the use of blood products.

Two criteria give life to and delimit autonomy: informed consent and competence. Informed consent requires a physician to lay out all of the information a patient needs to have to understand a particular treatment—what the treatment itself will involve and what risks come with it. Only then can the patient exercise true autonomy. If a proposed treatment carries more risk than we think acceptable, we reserve the right to refuse it.

Often it is difficult for physicians to provide the information necessary for informed consent. Some treatments have proved useful, but how and why they work remain a mystery. Whether they will work for a particular patient cannot always be anticipated. Further, physicians have their own biases about preferred treatment. For example, there is now lively debate about coronary bypass surgery: how it stacks up against other forms of treatment, which patients make the best candidates for the surgery, whether the procedure is overused. The debate erupts, in part, because of sparse scientific data. Despite the fact that coronary bypass surgery was introduced in 1968, physicians await long-range studies that provide solid guidelines for calculating the risks and benefits of the surgery as it is performed today.

The principle of autonomy often goes head-to-head with the principle of beneficence. Those whose aim is to act in a beneficent manner often risk becoming paternalistic instead. Rather than respecting your autonomy, the paternalist assumes that you do not have the capacity to make a decision that is in your best interest and steps in to make the decision for you. When physicians had nothing to offer their patients but comfort and care, there was little room for paternalism. But as medicine as an art gave way to biomedicine, paternalism became an increasingly frequent interloper. Physicians' desire to do good, linked with specialization and improved medical understanding, increased the risk of paternalistic judgments.

There are many instances when informed consent cannot be honored at all. In emergencies, when time is of the essence and the patient's views are unknown, treatment is begun at once on the assumption that the patient would want aggressive treatment. Exceptions to informed consent have also been made on what is called the therapeutic privilege. When a physician believes that a patient, depressed or unstable or frightened, might be harmed by a complete and honest medical assessment, therapeutic privilege is used to justify withholding information. The use of therapeutic privilege is in decline, however. Many now hold that there are few, if any, cases in which it can be justified.

Informed consent, essential to autonomy, is meaningless if the individual is not competent to make decisions. Children, the retarded, the mentally ill, and the comatose are considered incompetent to make decisions for themselves. But competence is not always so clear-cut. Many people are highly competent in all but one situation—think of people so frightened by an event that, like deer frozen in a car's headlights, they are unable even to move. Many are competent at one time or another—think of elderly people who drift in and out of periods of confusion. Ethicists Tom Beauchamp and James Childress suggest the following tests for incompetence:

1. Inability to offer a preference
2. Inability to grasp the situation
3. Inability to understand information
4. Inability to give a reason
5. Inability to give a rational reason
6. Inability to give risk/benefit reasons
7. Inability to reach a reasonable decision (judged by what a reasonable person would decide).[8]

Clear and straightforward, the tests are nonetheless only a guide. Each patient has his or her own abilities, outlooks, idiosyncrasies, bundled up with anxiety. Each physician has his or her own standard for what constitutes adequate capacity to make decisions about one's medical care.

The addition of justice and autonomy as ethical principles alongside beneficence and nonmaleficence helped solve some of the problems that came with biomedicine. But there were many other problems. Embedded in the fabric of our culture, those problems gave rise to bioethics. It is a young field, its opening generally dated between 1969, with the founding of the Hastings Center, and 1971, with the founding of the Kennedy Institute of Ethics. Bioethics grapples with the problems in medicine and the life sciences that are not simply scientific.

The number of bioethical issues is growing exponentially. Even if bioethics enables us to arrive at some consensus about the problems that face us now, more problems are sure to come with the future. Every new technology creates new problems, for our understanding of what any technology can and cannot do is formed as we use—and misuse—that technology. So, too, will new diseases give rise to new bioethical issues. Think how AIDS has altered our perception of disease, medicine, and our responsibilities to others. Our right to health care is increasingly reined in by our own or our society's ability to pay. Now we have arrived at the point where we cannot pay for all that we have the ability to do. Deciding what will be made available will be a struggle for all of us. As potential patients—beneficiaries of medicine—we will want all that we can have. As taxpayers—benefactors of medicine—we will want only as much as justice requires.

Cultural changes also raise new bioethical issues. Over time our ideas about health itself have changed. Increasingly, health has come to mean much more than normal functioning of the body and freedom from disease. As defined by the United Nations World Health Organization, health is "a state of complete physical, mental, and social well-being and not merely the absence of disease or infirmity."[9] It is a stunning definition. Carried to its logical conclusion, every social action concerns health.

Our ideas about who controls health have also changed. Not so very long ago people believed that health was determined by the Fates, God, nature, or dumb luck. Today people tend to believe that they themselves, in partnership with biomedicine's practitioners, are ultimately in charge. Thomas Donaldson provided one bizarre example. In 1990 he sought the court's permission for physicians to freeze him, then sever and store his head. He reasoned that when science had a cure for his cancer and a technique for brain transplantation, his brain could be implanted in another body and he could get on with the rest of his life.[10]

Finally, views of human potential, rights, and obligations are ever evolving. As these are codified in legislation, regulation, and legal decisions, new issues will become apparent.

The gush of medical technology is so recent and so overwhelming that we are only beginning to recognize its concomitant social and moral implications. We scramble to take our bearings while being run helter-skelter into the future. The new medical technology has even called into question our most fundamental belief in the ultimate value of life. As it is understood in the field of bioethics, vitalism—the belief that everything should be done to preserve life, whatever its condition—often seems downright pernicious today. Ethicist Joseph Fletcher, believing it no longer serves us well, holds that

> the traditional ethics based on the sanctity of life—which was the classical doctrine of medical idealism in its pre-scientific phases—must give way to a code of ethics of the quality of life. This comes about for humane reasons. It is a result of modern medicine's successes, not failures.[11]

UNDERSTANDING OURSELVES

The whole is very often more than the sum of its parts—certainly that is true of human beings. But to understand the whole, one must scrutinize the parts. Medicine has progressed in just this fashion. Over the centuries physicians have trained their vision on increasingly small details. Bone and muscle, organs, physiological systems, cells—by better understanding these, physicians have adjusted and enlarged their understanding of the whole human being. A part of the body can say much about the whole. For example, using a simple blood test, a physician might figure out what ails a listless patient.

Considering medicine's methodology, it is not surprising that in 1985 Robert Sinsheimer, a biochemist, proposed that the scientific community make a concerted, coordinated effort to map the human genome. A genome is the set of genetic instructions by which a particular life-form is constructed and functions. Packed into every nucleated cell (blood cells have no nucleus) are chromosomes, strands of deoxyribonucleic acid—DNA, for short. Chromosomes, in turn, are composed of genes. Each gene is a single protein responsible for a particular biological activity. All together, the genes represent the recipe for an individual.

The fundamental unit of DNA is a pair of nitrogenous bases, either adenine (A) connected to thymine (T) or cytosine (C) connected to guanine (G). Lined up one after another, the base pairs form the rungs of the ladderlike DNA strands. In the course of cell division, DNA splits down the middle. Because the bases are complementary, each half can correctly reassemble the other half.

Proteins are made of amino acids. All told, there are only twenty amino acids, each of which is referred to by a particular set of three bases. Reading the letters—A, T, C, and G— along either side of the DNA strand is like reading a recipe; it shows what amino acids are put together in what order to make a certain protein. The paucity of amino acids is no hindrance for nature. Consider this analogy: "The system may be thought of as a Tinkertoy set, in which sticks, wheels and blades can be snapped together into windmills, castles, cars and a diversity of other forms limited only by the child's imagination and patience."[1] The entire sequence of bases for one protein forms a gene. Each has a specific location, or locus, on one specific chromosome.

The magnitude of an effort to map the human genome is breathtaking. The DNA for a simple yeast plant consists of fifteen million base pairs. The DNA for human beings is thought to consist of some three billion base pairs segmented into one hundred thousand genes. Scientists have a good idea of the locus for about twenty-seven hundred genes.[2] But so far just a few genes have been decoded. Now, with machines to sequence the base pairs and computers to roam through the sequencing for clues to the codes, the pace will surely quicken. Still, in contemplating the genome project, it was estimated that the effort would take fifteen years and cost $3 billion.

An understanding of the human genome offers tantalizing prospects. Considerably more than 99 percent of our DNA is the same in every human being; the hereditary differences that make each of us unique are determined by variations in less than 1 percent of our DNA.[3] The list of rare diseases, like hemophilia, known to be transmitted genetically has more than three thousand entries, and the list will grow as more genes are isolated and located.

Further, there is solid evidence that genes can cause or make us vulnerable to many common diseases, like diabetes, heart disease, and cancer. An ability to read the genome would dramatically alter the practice of medicine. Now patients present themselves when they are clearly sick. In the future, physicians could pretreat their patients for illness or a high risk of illness predicted by a reading of their genome. As such, medicine would be used as a preventive, rather than curative, tool.

A knowledge of the human genome could serve as the reference for the development of proteins with which to counter many diseases. More important, a knowledge of the human genome opens the door to gene therapy. One form of therapy sends an engineered virus laden with the healthy gene to a patient's cells. There it inserts the good DNA into the cells, which will then begin producing the essential protein. This is somatic-cell repair, correction of a defect by alteration of the patient's body cells. Germ-cell repair is a form of gene therapy involving the insertion of a correctly functioning gene into sex cells. As envisioned now, this would be done on an embryo when it has only four or eight cells. Or it may occur as a by-product of attempts at somatic-cell gene therapy. Repair of this sort will affect not only the child that develops from that embryo; all of its children, and the generations that arise from them, will be affected, too.

Scientists believe that each of us carries at least three lethal genetic defects in a recessive state. Indeed, one in every twenty-five people carries the gene for cystic fibrosis,[4] a disease that causes the production of a gummy mucus that clogs and ultimately destroys the lungs. Carriers are not afflicted by the genetic defect, but their children could be if the other parent is also a carrier. Who could—would—resist the urge to use gene therapy to repair the DNA of a child with cystic fibrosis?

An understanding of the human genome could catapult biomedicine to an entirely new orbit. The potential benefits are plain to see. Even if they were not, sheer curiosity made the project hard to resist. "How can we not do it? We used to think our fate was in the stars," observes James Watson, who with Francis Crick figured out the structure of DNA in 1953. "Now we know, in large measure, our fate is in our genes."[5]

The intense excitement within the scientific community was contagious. Congress anted up $53 million in 1989 alone.[6] The illustrious Watson was appointed project director. And in the fall of 1990 the first attempt was made to use gene therapy for a four-year-old with adenosine deaminase deficiency, a rare disorder of the immune system. (Ten months later the child's physicians were delighted with their patient's progress.) All in all, the genome project had an auspicious beginning. In 1992 the project lost some of its luster when the National Institutes of Health applied for patents on almost three thousand genes identified in their labs. Some scientists were aghast; patenting is contrary to the tradition of scientific inquiry. Others maintained that patenting was essential; without it, companies would not have the exclusive rights needed to protect their investment in developing a gene. Watson felt so strongly that patenting was wrong that he resigned his position, but around the world, work on deciphering the human genome continues at a furious pace.

The genome project's downside continues to nag. Many scientists were dubious when the project was first suggested. Many remain so. Some doubt that it can really be done. Others fret that it will monopolize science, drawing researchers and funding from other important areas of inquiry. Still others wonder if it should be pursued at all, they worry that the knowledge gleaned from the project will add still more to a heap of unresolved ethical problems.

Just locating defective genes is fraught with ethical problems. Amniocentesis and chorionic villi assay, two kinds of prenatal testing for genetic defects, have led many parents to seek abortions, which many others deem ethically abhorrent. Abortions performed because of the presence of a genetic disorder in the fetus will likely increase as more genes are isolated and located. Greater knowledge of the genome may also have a subtle effect on the directions medical research takes. Consider Tay-Sachs disease. Infants born with the disorder develop properly until about six months, then stall, begin declining, and slowly, inevitably die by about age four. Once the gene for Tay-Sachs was located, vigorous information and genetic-counseling programs were set up. Because the disease appeared mostly among children of eastern European Jewish background, the programs were focused on the Jewish community. Prenatal testing, which showed if the fetus had Tay-Sachs disease, gave parents who are carriers the ability to abort those fetuses that were affected. Adults who were carriers and disapproved of abortion could consider not having children or adopting children. So successful were these programs that now the incidence of Tay-Sachs disease is lower among those of eastern European Jewish ancestry than in the general public. At the same time, funds for medical research on how to treat children with Tay-Sachs have dwindled. Why, after all, fund research for a vanishing population of patients?

In comparison, scientists are only now closing in on the gene for cystic fibrosis. Knowing that it is a genetic disease but unable to spot it with prenatal testing, physicians had pursued aggressive treatment of the disease's victims and have succeeded in raising average life expectancy. In 1960 the likelihood that a child with cystic fibrosis would live to start kindergarten was slim. Between 1980 and 1991, median life expectancy rose from nineteen years of age to twenty-nine.[7] Scientists have used gene therapy to cure cystic fibrosis cells in the laboratory, and they expect that one day they will be able to use it on actual patients. Nonetheless, past experience suggests that forms of treatment other than gene therapy could be developed to give those with cystic fibrosis a full life span.

What about genetic diseases that are deadly but do not preclude a meaningful life? Huntington's disease is one. Dormant until sometime between the ages of thirty and fifty, it then manifests itself in the loss of voluntary muscular control and intellectual capacity, killing slowly, surely, gruesomely. What would you do if a prenatal test showed that your unborn child had the gene for Huntington's disease? A case might be made for aborting a fetus with Tay-Sachs disease, which kills so early in life. A case might be made for aborting a fetus with cystic fibrosis, which cramps all of its victim's relatively short life. Can a case similarly be made for aborting a fetus with Huntington's disease, which first declares itself only in middle age?

A decision to abort that fetus suggests that our desire for perfection and long life has grown so fanatical that a good first thirty years or more of life are of no real value. Abortion in such a case would also make a statement about you, the parent with the defective gene: This disease is trouble with a capital *T,* and had the technology been available before your birth, you would have been aborted. Some worry that society will come to demand that the unborn who have the gene for Huntington's disease or the like be aborted, even if the parents think abortion is immoral.

Many believe that postnatal testing for a genetic abnormality is unethical if you have no cure for the disease. Newborns are tested for phenylketonuria (PKU), the inability to metabolize the amino acid phenylalanine. Early knowledge of its presence is vital. A genetic disease, it can be controlled by diet. Untreated, it causes severe retardation. Testing programs for sickle-cell anemia, however, initially proved more destructive than constructive. There was at that time little or no treatment for the disease, which affects blood cells and is found predominantly among blacks. Moreover, because of the widespread confusion about the trait and the disease, many who were found to be carriers, even though they did not have the disease, lost their jobs and were charged more for insurance. Currently there is no cure for Huntington's disease. Nor are there treatments that can blunt the effects of the disease, as there are for cystic fibrosis. Finally, in the case of testing for Huntington's disease, how does one live the symptom-free first part of one's life with the knowledge of sure impending doom?

One might somehow manage to live a full and meaningful symptom-free first part of life, but that task, difficult in itself, might become impossible if employers or insurance companies got wind of what one's genetic profile discloses. Huntington's disease, even the possibility of cancer or high blood pressure—these are problems that society and its institutions steer clear of. Knowing something about the future, who will hire you, who will sell you life insurance?

Once mastered, gene therapy may offer a way around many medical problems. But the potential hazards of gene therapy itself raise a swarm of ethical questions. Anxiety about the creation and escape of unanticipated, perhaps lethal viruses designed to slip healthy DNA into the patient is real. Gene therapy on sex cells causes concern because the alterations, beneficial and deleterious alike, will be carried down through all succeeding generations without reversal.

Actual surgery on cellular material, still further out on the horizon, would entail pulling off immensely intricate surgery without a single misstep. However gene therapy is done, new genetic material must be inserted correctly. It is easy to see how a single slip could produce disaster. Even gene therapy that succeeds in what is intended might spark unexpected, devastating side effects. What will we do with the mishaps? Because the risks are theoretical, no patient could give truly informed consent, at least in the beginning of such venturing. Even if an individual accepts the risk, will society as a whole also go along? When experimentation on one person could ravage entire populations, even the human species as a whole, the case can be made for requiring society's informed consent.

Gene therapy gives pause to many even as a concept. Some oppose gene therapy because they oppose any human manipulation of our own genetic material. For those who view life as a divine gift, gene therapy is a dramatic example of playing God. Others come to essentially the same conclusion but for different reasons. They worry that a full-blown program of gene therapy to eliminate genetic disorders might at the same time radically alter the gene pool—the aggregate of genetic information carried by an entire population. If its gene pool is diminished, the human species may be less flexible and thus less able to adapt to changes in the environment. They warn that the changes we make in our own bodies represent changes in our overall ecology. That might disastrously upset the balance of nature and redirect its course. One change in the gene pool will precipitate other changes that we cannot anticipate. We understand the idea of the ripple effect, but we have not mastered the art of forecasting it. One has only to look at the rancorous debate on the greenhouse effect and its consequences, all set in motion by our use of fossil fuels. A sterling example of the complexity and unpredictability of ecological changes, it has caused vociferous argument among scientists, who debate not only how grave the problem is but also how the greenhouse effect will show itself. The scientific debate has in turn spilled into the political arena, as we fight over what to do now to stem changes that may or may not lie in the future. A similar debate could easily arise over the potential long-term effect of a simple genetic manipulation.

How gene therapy is applied will make a critical difference. If it is used to provide real therapy, the problem of abuse does not loom as large. Even so, there is no firm line separating the therapeutic from the nontherapeutic. Imagine that gene therapy allowed us to manipulate the genes for physical stature. Determining when shortness is a defect is at some point subjective. Many people who are not afflicted by dwarfism feel that shortness has profoundly constrained their aspirations. Four and a half feet tall, five feet tall, five and a half feet tall, six feet tall—where is the border between defective and normal? There you will find the line between therapeutic repair and a subjective enhancement.

Gene therapy lends itself to any number of other projects. Consider eugenics, the science of the improvement of a species by selective breeding, first advanced by Sir Francis Galton in 1869. Negative eugenics refers to the suppression of undesirable qualities in the species. Couples who forgo having children because they might pass on a genetic disorder are, knowingly or unknowingly, practicing negative eugenics. In the United States negative eugenics was codified in laws that permitted forced sterilization of people the state deemed defective—until 1971 Virginia had just such a law on its books. Positive eugenics is selective breeding of individuals with superior characteristics. In the late nineteenth century positive eugenics fueled exhortations to the upper classes that they have many, many children. An institutional expression of positive eugenics came in 1971, when Robert Graham established the Hermann J. Muller Repository for Germinal Choice. Those who wish to help in the betterment of the human species can supposedly use semen supplied by the repository to conceive fine children, for the semen is collected from Nobel laureates and other renowned scientists.

Positive eugenics is fundamental to today's livestock business. But human beings are not livestock. Eugenics might make for a better meat loaf, but there is no proof that it makes for a better human being. Critics point out that the child fathered by a Nobel laureate may prove utterly dull. Or perhaps the child will be intellectually bright but also a boor. Scientists note, too, that we have no way really to select for traits. Is musical ability a product only of the genotype— one's individual genetic makeup—or of the phenotype— one's genetic makeup overlaid and refined by the environment in which one develops? Still, those who are intrigued by eugenics will champion the mastery of gene therapy. By comparison, selective breeding is a hit-or-miss approach to improving the species.

Scientists also point out that what is viewed as a genetic issue might in fact be a social problem. Many societies strongly favor males. A study conducted in 1976–1977 at two hospitals in India where pregnant women were told the sex of the fetus found that 430 of 450 women who were carrying females chose to have an abortion.[8] Americans seem to have the same impulse, albeit muted. There are no studies on how often abortion for sex selection is requested. But if it is, the request might not be turned down. In a 1985 survey of 295 American geneticists, 34 percent said they would determine the fetus's sex for a couple who, having four daughters, would abort the fetus if it were female. Another 28 percent said they would refer the couple to someone who would provide the testing. Autonomy, the belief that family planning is appropriate, and the legality of abortion on demand were reasons given for their views.[9] But abortion because the fetus is not the desired sex seems brutish. One's sex is not a defect.

If abortion for sex selection troubles us, what are we to make of efforts to refine methods of sex predetermination? By this process, sperm carrying the Y chromosome, for males, are separated from those carrying the X chromosome, for females. Depending on which sex is desired, one or the other batch of sperm is inseminated in the woman, thereby obviating the need for abortion. Sex predetermination is perfectly acceptable to many. Everyone knows couples who have boy after boy or girl after girl. If a couple would like the experience of raising children of both sexes, what is wrong with helping them satisfy that longing? At the same time, society would benefit from a decline in the birth rate; couples would not be tempted to have more children than they would otherwise choose just because the next child might be the hoped-for sex. Those who favor the use of sex predetermination acknowledge that, yes, at first the ratio of males to females might increase. But they feel sure that the ratio would soon return to normal.

Feminist Gena Corea believes that sex predetermination would create a permanent scarcity of females, with disastrous consequences. She predicts a rise in crime, homosexuality, and prostitution. Females would rarely be the firstborn child, enjoying the benefits studies have shown come to the first-born. Further, women in such a society would be pressured to marry—perhaps even to have several husbands at one time—and to bear children.

Corea's dark forebodings about the insidious consequences of sex predetermination seem farfetched to many who nonetheless oppose the technology. As they see it, choosing the sex of a child implies the propriety of what are sardonically called designer babies. One need not reject the idea that humans can and should have control over their lives to reject control in this area. What does such a practice say about a parent's willingness to accept rather than control a child's individuality? In what ways other than being the "right" sex would such a made-to-specification child have to satisfy his or her parent?

The concern that we might easily drift from therapeutic uses of gene therapy to more frivolous uses is real and valid. Although gene therapy is for the most part still off in the future, many point to the explosion of reproductive technologies as proof positive of our inclination to stray beyond thoughtful, responsible, ethical applications of technology.

The impulse to procreate is a very basic, very strong desire in human beings. Not surprisingly, infertility is a profoundly frustrating and dispiriting problem. Further, it is not such a rare problem. Two British researchers believe that "one quarter of all the women who attempt to conceive experience an episode of subfertility at some stage in their reproductive life."[10]

The new medical technology has done much to solve those problems. Gains in understanding the delicate biochemistry by which conception takes place and embryonic and fetal development proceeds have come at a rapid pace. Fertility specialists now have many strategies by which to encourage conception and sustain a pregnancy. For many couples the obstacle is getting egg and sperm together. For them fertility specialists use one of two technologies.

The first is artificial insemination, the placement of semen, aswarm with sperm, in the woman's vagina, cervical canal, or uterus by means of a syringe. Artificial insemination is used to bypass inhospitable mucus in the woman's vagina; deliver semen of impotent men; or, by combining several collections of semen, increase the chances of men with low sperm counts to father a child. The second, very much more complicated process is called in vitro fertilization (IVF). IVF is custom-made for women with blocked fallopian tubes, which form a barrier between egg and sperm. Eggs, or ova, are removed from the ovaries in a surgical procedure called laparoscopy, fertilized with sperm in a petri dish, and then surgically placed in the uterus for implantation and gestation.

Artificial insemination is not a new technology. Common only in this century, it was first used over two hundred years ago. Nor is it a high technology. Women have been known to inseminate themselves at home with a turkey baster. Not so with IVF. IVF research is very young. Every aspect of this technically demanding process requires that it be confined to the scientific setting.

The early research on IVF had many goals. The research gave scientists the opportunity to observe fertilization, until then tucked away in the tubes. The effectiveness of antifertility drugs; the fertilizability of ova produced by women who were for some reason infertile; the biochemistry of embryos of couples in which the woman had a history of spontaneous abortion; the effect of teratogens—external agents, like chemicals—on embryos; the mechanism by which chromosomal abnormalities, like Down's syndrome, occur; normal and abnormal cell growth—these were purposes of IVF research above and beyond its use as a technology to bring about conception and pregnancy in women with damaged fallopian tubes.

The Roman Catholic church immediately expressed concern about the research, concern that was echoed by a larger public:

> No objective, even though noble in itself, such as a foreseeable advantage to science, to other human beings or to society, can in any way justify experimentation on living human embryos or fetuses, whether viable or not, either inside or outside the mother's womb. The informed consent ordinarily required for clinical experimentation on adults cannot be granted by the parents, who may not freely dispose of the physical integrity or life of the unborn child. Moreover, experimentation on embryos and fetuses always involves risk, and indeed in most cases it involves the certain expectation of harm to their physical integrity or even their death.
>
> To use human embryos or fetuses as the object or instrument of experimentation constitutes a crime against their dignity as human beings having a right to the same respect that is due to the child already born and to every human person.[11]

Although there were and are those who disagree with the Roman Catholic church's basic premise that the embryo or fetus is a human being and must be treated, like you and me, as a human being, concern about the use of embryos for such research prompted Congress to ban federally sponsored IVF research in 1974. The ban was lifted the next year, but the government has refused to provide any funding for the research because of continued strong moral opposition to the use of embryos as objects of experimentation. The experimental nature of all technologies early on in their development means that there are always risks—and unimagined risks at that. What might happen to an ovum or embryo in the course of manipulation? As with gene therapy, might there be a risk of creating another problem as one is solved? Also, a firm principle of experimentation is that subjects not be put at risk without their consent, but the potential child has no decision-making role in these situations. The church was not alone in seeing this, too, as ethically problematic.

The landscape changed dramatically in 1978, with the announcement from England of the birth of Louise Brown, the first child conceived in vitro—the first so-called test-tube baby. Couples who had sadly concluded that they would never conceive a child flocked to IVF programs that bloomed like flowers after a desert rain. By 1991, more than a decade after Louise Brown's birth, some ten thousand children conceived by IVF had been born just in the United States.[12] Time has shown there to be no greater incidence of congenital defects among them than in the population as a whole. As for long-term risks, it is too early to tell what those might be. However, some physicians expect to see high rates of cancer among women who tried IVF, which depends on powerful drugs to accelerate cell growth.

It is not just the experimental aspect of IVF that disturbs the Roman Catholic church. It has steadfastly, vehemently opposed any intervention in conception because of its artificiality. Procreation is no longer accomplished through loving sexual union.

For many, the church's concern about artificiality seems strained. Is the technology by which infertility can be overcome any less ethical than the technology by which the farsighted are able, by the artificiality of eyeglasses, to see more accurately? Every couple who have undergone the dreary process of infertility studies and any of the procedures for conception would agree that the inherent artificiality is unfortunate. But they stoutly maintain that artificiality is not a compelling ethical reason to invalidate the procedures.

Another ethical problem that arises from IVF concerns not misused embryos but unused embryos. Early on, the process of collecting an egg, fertilizing it, and placing it in the uterus involved a laborious process of tracking ovulation and, after that, two surgeries. As a consequence the success rate was very low, the cost very high. To improve chances of the entire procedure's success, a course of drug treatment to boost the number of eggs released at ovulation was added at the beginning of the IVF procedure. By this so-called superovulation, physicians were regularly able to retrieve as many as eight eggs at one time. But how is this wealth of eggs to be handled? If all are fertilized and placed in the uterus and if all of the embryos implant, the mother will wind up with eight fetuses. These cannot develop properly or sufficiently, because the mother cannot support that number of fetuses. The physician could use some of the embryos and throw out the rest. Or all of the embryos could be placed in the mother's uterus; if too many implanted, the physician could perform fetal reduction—the antiseptic term for selective abortion of some of the fetuses to allow the others to reach viability or come closer to full term and normal delivery. That, of course, can be seen as the sacrifice of one life for another.

Embryo freezing, mastered several years after IVF began

to be used as a therapy, reduced the risk that one might have to consider fetal reduction. Some of the fertilized embryos are frozen, to be thawed and returned to the uterus at a later time. The upshot is that a number of embryos might never be used. After some successful tries with in vitro fertilization, a couple could decide that they have quite enough children. Is it right to throw out the unused embryos?

Some embryos have been orphaned. The most well known case is that of Mario and Elsa Rios, a wealthy couple who had placed two embryos in an embryo bank, then died in an airplane crash. What is to be the fate of orphaned embryos? Should they be thrown out? Should they be adopted by a couple who are unable to conceive because they have no egg or sperm? If they are adopted, what claims do they have on their genetic parents' estates?

Frozen embryos have also become the subject of divorce cases. Mary Sue and Junior Lewis Davis were enrolled in an IVF program. Seven ova were gathered and fertilized, then frozen in the hope that by introducing them to her uterus at the height of Mary Sue's next ovulation, prospects for a pregnancy would brighten.

In the meantime the Davises' marriage came apart. Mary Sue went to court to gain custody of the embryos. "I feel pretty strongly," she said, and went on to explain: "I'm not bitter toward him, but I think he is acting very selfish. I personally see the embryo as a living thing, and I think I have more rights as the mother."[13]

Junior Davis asserted that the embryos were not alive, that they were simply joint property. He did not want children with his genetic contribution brought into the world under these circumstances. A lower court accepted Mary Sue Davis's claim, but the decision was reversed on appeal.

The slippery slope, the thin edge of the wedge, the camel's nose under the edge of the tent—all are metaphors for the idea that one thing leads to another. The rationalization for loosening one prohibition will soon be used to rationalize the loosening of other prohibitions until, before you know it, the very core of a principle has been violated. In reply, many quote the Latin saying *abusus non tollit usum*—that something can be abused does not mean that it should not be used.

In vitro fertilization, like most other technologies, raises concerns about where it might lead. The reverence for human life demands that we recognize the intrinsic worth of every human being. But many who do not believe in the value, the humanness, of the embryo are nonetheless disturbed by IVF. To them the technology bespeaks an attitude that treats the embryo as a mere tool—a means to an end. Others feel that too easy acceptance of in vitro fertilization threatens the ideal of an emotionally and biologically united family. Some couples have applied to IVF programs wanting the procedure but with donated egg or sperm. Unhappy with their looks or intelligence, they did not wish to pass on those characteristics. What such parents cannot avoid passing on are the problems that flow from their devastated sense of self-esteem as individuals and as a couple.

Sperm banks, developed in the 1960s, were initially established to keep frozen semen collections for men who plan to have a vasectomy but want what has been called fertility insurance. If for some reason they later decide they want more children, they can withdraw the semen and use it for artificial insemination. Sperm banks are also used by men who need medical treatment—for example, radiation for cancer—that might permanently destroy their ability to produce healthy sperm. But before long, sperm banks began accepting semen collections for donation to couples in which the man, for whatever reason, cannot supply the sperm necessary for conception.

Artificial insemination with donated sperm (AID—sometimes called donor insemination so as not to be confused with the disease AIDS) is an altogether different kettle of fish. Because a woman is inseminated with semen that is not her husband's, some see AID as a form of adultery pure and simple. Many dismiss as nonsense the description of this medical procedure as adultery, but they are disturbed by the fact that a family so enlarged depends on the genetic union of one member of the couple and a stranger. Others warn that it allows women to become dangerously free agents. What if a woman uses AID to get around a husband who does not want another child? What if single women use it as a way to have children without having a marriage? Indeed, many lesbians have used artificial insemination to have children. Further, the relations between contemporary American men and women have been strained by the feminist movement, and of late a significant number of heterosexual women, unable to find a man with whom to share a life, have chosen AID as a way to have children anyway. Marriage might elude them, but parenthood would not.

Many see a beneficent side to AID. If a husband has no sperm or if he has a genetic disease that militates against his procreating, he and his wife can still have a child that has at least the wife's genetic contribution. They can also have the profound experience of pregnancy and birth. There are other advantages as well. Artificial insemination using donated sperm obviates the need for adoption, a process that is expensive and, because of abortion and the rising number of unwed mothers who choose to keep their children, increasingly difficult.

Are these new technologies reflections of a sorry human tendency? Ethicist David Smith observes:

I do not mean to imply that artificial insemination by donor (AID) or the conception of test-tube babies are wrong because a technician serves as a middleman. . . . I mean to suggest that somewhere on this technological ladder . . . we move from an attitude that facilitates humility and loyalty in reproduction to one that refuses to live with the sterile, imperfect or unknown. And I think that to be a fateful and unfortunate moment.[14]

Of all the new forms of procreation, perhaps the best known and most discussed is surrogate motherhood. In surrogacy a woman carries a child for another couple, to whom she turns the child over upon birth.

In 1984 Mary Beth Whitehead read an ad for women interested in surrogacy. The mother of two children, she had enjoyed her pregnancies and thought that surrogacy offered her a good way to help a couple who could not bear children. And so she applied to, and was accepted by, the program run by Noel Keane, a lawyer who had come to specialize in the business of matching surrogates with couples who were unable to have children. Whitehead signed a contract by which she agreed to be inseminated with William Stern's semen and carry the child to birth. Because there were no laws pertaining to surrogacy, adoption laws would be used; Whitehead would terminate her parental rights, and Elizabeth Stern would then adopt the child.

Keane's services did not come cheap. His share was $10,000. Whitehead would receive $10,000 upon the delivery of a live, healthy baby. But in the case of Whitehead and the Sterns, the financial costs were trifling compared with the emotional costs. Their deal went awry when Whitehead fell in love with her baby. She and her husband fled with their two children and the baby girl in a desperate attempt to keep the infant. They were found by the police in Florida, and the baby was taken back to New Jersey, where the Sterns took custody of her. The Whiteheads went home to New Jersey and began the long legal battle to regain the child.

The mystique of motherhood, along with the biological fact that it is the mother, not the father, who carries and bears a child, was for many a justification of Whitehead's stronger claim to the child. Here the term *surrogacy* was a misnomer. Whitehead was no stand-in. She was the child's genetic, as well as gestational, mother.

To weaken that claim, others pointed out that Whitehead had signed a contract to act as a surrogate for the Sterns. A deal is a deal, they insisted. Further, the Sterns could offer Baby M, as the baby was referred to in the course of the legal proceedings, a better life. The Whiteheads' marriage was shaky—indeed, during the legal battle the Whiteheads separated and later divorced. Richard Whitehead had had problems with alcoholism, and neither had any higher education. Richard Whitehead was a garbage collector, and Mary Beth Whitehead had at one time been a go-go dancer. In contrast, the Sterns were professionals, she a pediatrician and he a biochemist. Their marriage appeared strong and calm. The Sterns could give the child a richer environment—richer intellectually and monetarily. The argument over who would be better parents was carried to the absurd when a psychologist, Marshall Schecter, testifying as an expert witness, said that Whitehead was not a good mother because she had not played pattycake properly. Instead of clapping at the end of the rhyme, she had said, "Hooray!"

Harvey Sorkow, the lower court judge who first heard the case, ruled that Whitehead's contract with the Sterns was valid and enforceable. He terminated Whitehead's parental rights and immediately carried out adoption proceedings by which Elizabeth Stern became the child's mother. The case was immediately appealed to the New Jersey Supreme Court, which ruled that Whitehead's parental rights could not be terminated against her will, and while custody of Baby M remained with the Sterns, Whitehead was given visitation rights.

The case, closely covered by a swarm of reporters from media across the country, was arresting. Many people had been unaware that surrogacy even existed, and while the medical technology—artificial insemination—by which this surrogacy was effected is neither high-tech nor new, the very idea of surrogacy was foreign and unsettling. What was new was the open, high-finance deal making surrounding surrogacy, a crass challenge to age-old assumptions about what makes a family a family. Hilary Hanafan, a psychologist who works with surrogate mothers, plumbs the public's bemusement:

> I think surrogate parenting . . . really is a direct threat to each individual's notion about their own relationship with their mother. . . . Surrogate parenting is a very threatening concept in the sense that it questions whether or not a mother's attachment to her child is absolute.[15]

That class was so manifestly a part of the arguments about who would be better parents for Baby M gave credence to the charges made by opponents of surrogacy. They see surrogacy as nothing more than baby selling. They hold that the fees paid to surrogates are simply a means of exploiting women who need money, and they envision a society in which the rich pay the poor to serve as baby factories. When all is said and done, the $10,000 a surrogate might earn for bearing a child is a pittance.

Feminists, looking at surrogacy not so much as rich versus poor but as men versus women, are divided about surrogacy. Many assert that it is yet another way to demean women by placing them in a mechanistic role. They worry that surrogacy will come to be used by couples in which the wife views pregnancy as inconvenient, scary, risky. Indeed, Elizabeth Stern was not infertile. She chose surrogacy on the assumption that a self-diagnosed case of multiple sclerosis might be exacerbated by a pregnancy.

That surrogacy can spell misery for all the participants is amply demonstrated by the Baby M case, but there are many women who have been surrogates and have found the process rewarding. "It's a gift to be able to give others the same joy of a child that my husband and I have in our son," one surrogate said.[16] They reject the view that surrogacy should be banned, pointing out that prohibiting it demeans women because any restrictions are (paternalistically) predicated on the idea that women are not intelligent enough to decide how they will run their own lives, make their own happiness. And they reject the notion that this is nothing more than baby selling, a desperate gambit for women financially up against the wall. The fees paid to surrogates are perfectly appropriate recompense for their work. "The money is not the most important thing," one surrogate explained, "but it has let me stay home and be a full-time mother, which is very rewarding."[17]

In another form of surrogacy the surrogate is only the gestational mother. If a woman has ovaries but no uterus, she and her husband can use IVF to create an embryo, which is then implanted in the uterus of a woman who is willing to carry the child to birth. That was what Mark and Crispina Calvert did, but Anna Johnson, their surrogate, eventually balked, just as Mary Beth Whitehead had. In the ensuing custody suit, a California judge ruled in favor of the Calverts. Further, Johnson was not given visitation rights. Is Johnson's case truly weaker because, as the judge pointed out, unlike Whitehead, she was not also the genetic mother?

Suppose a couple wanting a child arrange for the creation of an embryo from donated egg and donated sperm, to be placed in the uterus of yet another woman for gestation. Whose claim to be the mother is the strongest? How shall we rank all these forms of motherhood? By any reckoning, the procreative technologies have led to a mind-boggling array of possible mother-child relationships. A child can have three mothers: a genetic mother, the woman who provided the ovum; a gestational mother, the woman who nurtured the child in her womb before birth; and a social mother, the woman who raises the child.

Who is the child's true mother? Feminist Barbara Katz Rothman believes pregnancy is the key:

> Any pregnant woman is the mother of the child she bears. Her gestational relationship establishes motherhood. We will not accept the idea that we can look at a woman, heavy with child, and say the child is not hers. The fetus is part of the woman's body, regardless of the source of the egg and sperm.[18]

By Rothman's standard, Mary Beth Whitehead and Anna Johnson were ill-treated by the judicial system; they are the true mothers of the children they bore. Extrapolating from Rothman's standard, Mary Sue Davis's claim that she has more rights than Junior Davis to their embryos, frozen in an IVF clinic, is wrong. It is a biological fact that pregnancy makes the mother and father unequal contributors to the creation of their child, but Davis was never pregnant.

The overarching issues that arise from surrogacy and AID concern the meaning of a child and the meaning of the family. Critics of surrogacy point out that the fee paid to the surrogate is not for services but for a healthy baby. Whitehead's contract provided for payment of only $1,000 if the baby was stillborn. Further, the contract gave the Sterns the right to demand that Whitehead have an abortion if prenatal testing indicated that the fetus was in any way less than perfect. What are the children of these arrangements? Are they the expression of our reverence for and delight in life, or are they mere goods in a commercial transaction?

Many people believe that surrogacy and AID allow parenthood to slip from its essential mooring in the family. They worry that a subtle dynamic can come into play between parents who do not have a parallel relationship to their child. If the adorable baby has an obstreperous adolescence, will one parent find it easy to wash his or her hands of the problem, charging, "This child isn't mine"? And what of the covenant of marriage, by which people bind themselves together in a relationship of emotional and sexual constancy? Ethicist Paul Ramsey believes that that covenant is violated by procreative techniques that provide a husband and wife with only an illusion of true genetic parenthood:

Most Protestants, and nowadays a great many Catholics, endorse contraceptive devices which separate the sex *act* as an act of love from whatever tendency there may be in the act . . . toward the engendering of a child. But they do *not* separate the sphere or realm of their personal love from the sphere or realm of their procreation, nor do they distinguish between *the person* with whom the bond of love is nourished and *the person* with whom procreation may be brought into exercise.[19]

Joseph Fletcher disagrees. Constancy in marriage, Fletcher asserts, is not necessarily defined by constancy in procreation. It is love, not genes, that gives parenthood its meaning and richness. His defense of AID holds as well for surrogacy: "Insemination from a donor is not adultery if marriage fidelity is conceived . . . to be a personal rather than a merely legal relationship."[20]

The technology that can change the way we conceive, carry, and bear children is itself in its infancy. The future may well provide us with artificial wombs. Considering the emotional entanglements that come with surrogacy, that would be a boon for women who have ovaries that can produce eggs but no womb that can shelter and nurture the unborn. It would also be handy for, say, a model who wants children but does not want to lose her figure during a pregnancy. Some scientists maintain that it is theoretically possible for a man to give birth. Like women who have given up on marriage but not parenthood, men could use artificial insemination with donated ova to become single parents. The future may also provide us with cloning—asexual reproduction. In cloning, the nucleus of an ovum is removed and replaced by a somatic cell. The resulting child would have the same genetic code as the person from whom the somatic cell came— a pleasing prospect for eugenicists and narcissists. But bypassing the sexual union, cloning would also deprive the clone of any model for commitment and responsibility to a uniquely other individual, spouse or child. Cloning smacks of a parent's inability to go beyond the self. How we respond to the ethical questions that the currently available and the potential technologies pose will describe our views about the purpose and worth of marriage and the family, as well as the purpose and worth of the individual.

BIOETHICS AT THE
END OF LIFE

It's not the being dead that frightens me; it's the dying."[1] So said the pseudonymous Emily Bauer, who was, by inches, dying of amyotrophic lateral sclerosis. It is a fact that the new medical technology, with its many interventionist treatments and forms of life support, often makes dying a more protracted process than it once was.

Biomedicine has sometimes moved ahead by spectacular, high-flying attempts at what seems the impossible. Consider this description of a forerunner of today's organ transplantation:

Human courage and compassion, not science, motivated three young surgeons in Boston to stitch a fresh cadaver kidney onto the arm of their acutely uremic and comatosed patient in 1947. This was done on the back ward of the Peter Bent Brigham Hospital using gooseneck lamps. The kidney immediately began to produce urine. Over the next couple of days, until it was rejected and lost function, the kidney cleared the uremic waste from the patient's blood stream and cleared her uremic symptoms. The experience with the transplanted kidney was just enough to allow her own kidneys to regain function and that individual left the hospital well.[2]

It is a miracle story. Other miracle stories are not as flamboyant; but under the surface they are just as dramatic. The polio vaccine, the product of dogged research, is but one example of biomedicine defeating a disease once thought unconquerable. Biomedicine can also preempt disease. For example, new surgery to ream out clogged carotid arteries has given life to individuals otherwise destined for strokes.

The so-called respirator, developed in the early 1960s, is one of the new medical technologies that have profoundly changed the practice of medicine. It is, properly speaking, a ventilator because it merely delivers air to the lungs. Respiration is the interaction of oxygen and tissue. If lung tissue is injured—for example, by pneumonia—it cannot transfer oxygen to the blood and remove carbon dioxide. But as long as lung tissue continues to work, ventilators can move air in and out of the lungs, enabling blood to flow and organs to remain alive.

The ventilator is one of the most valuable tools physicians can wield in their efforts to save life. Even people who are able to breathe on their own are often put on a ventilator because it gives the body a chance to rest and heal. When used by patients who cannot breathe, it stabilizes the body's physiology while physicians try to figure out what might be done. The ventilator can thus buy time: time to make the accurate, refined diagnoses that technology increasingly allows; time for treatment, which in itself can serve as a diagnostic tool—if a treatment is begun and the patient improves, that treatment has confirmed at least part of the problem.

The ventilator's role in the armory of life-support systems cannot be overestimated. But its role extends to the recent reexamination of the definition of death itself. Death has always been easily recognized: There is no heartbeat, and there is no breathing. If the heart stops, blood, with its essential cargo of oxygen, will not flow, and the brain will quickly die. If lung tissue is destroyed, the heart will be deprived of oxygen and will quickly die. If the whole brain is incapacitated, the heart will not pump.

The ventilator can sunder the interconnectedness of brain and body. It can keep blood coursing through a patient whose entire brain is dead. If the ventilator is turned off, heartbeat and respiration cease. If the ventilator is turned on again, heartbeat and respiration resume. So it was that physicians found themselves caring for patients whose bodies, only by virtue of a ventilator, were still functioning.

In 1968 the Ad Hoc Committee of the Harvard Medical School to Examine the Definition of Brain Death proposed criteria for determining when a patient on a ventilator is dead. The patient is tested for unreceptivity and unresponsivity. There are no spontaneous movements, no breathing, and no reflexes. The physician must make sure that what seems to be an irreversible coma is not in fact a result of hypothermia (low body temperature) or drug intoxication, and all of the tests must be repeated at least twenty-four hours later to confirm the diagnosis. These tests can be validated by a flat electroencephalogram, but they need not be. The clinical criteria are considered sufficient in themselves.

The Ad Hoc Committee's work was extremely unsettling to many people. Some saw it as an effort to redefine death. Having always equated the life of the body with the life of the person, many found it difficult to absorb what seemed a distinction between body death and brain death. The scientific terminology and the complexity of biological processes befuddled much of the public. Some believed that if the criteria for determining death were altered once, they might be altered any number of times in the future, leading to a slow but steady abandonment of the ancient concept of death. Further, it seemed an abandonment of the patient, whose body, thanks to the ventilator, was functioning, albeit by artificial means.

What most aroused concern, however, was the fact that the criteria were proposed just when organ transplantation had become increasingly successful. Indeed, surgeons were already attempting to transplant hearts that had just stopped beating. But ischemia, the anemia that results when blood flow stops, sets in very quickly, especially in the heart, spoiling tissue and making it unusable for transplantation. The Harvard criteria seemed a suspect device designed to increase the pool of organs available for donation. One ethicist pointed to "the paradox that the new definitions of death are proposed, at least in part, because they provide that certain parts of the newly defined dead body will be *less dead* than they would have been if the conventional definition were still used."[3]

The Ad Hoc Committee reiterated that the proposed criteria did not represent a new definition of death but rather the means for determining death when a ventilator is being used. Frankly acknowledging the dynamic of transplantation, the committee recommended that the physician certifying death not be associated with a potential organ recipient, thereby ensuring that the needs of someone awaiting a transplant were not coloring the determination of brain death.

The use of ventilators and other modern life-sustaining devices raises other ethical issues as well. For example, Emily Bauer clearly was not brain dead. She was on a ventilator because amyotrophic lateral sclerosis had robbed her of all muscle control. The ventilator was giving her more life, but the disease continued apace. Before long, Bauer rued the day she had gone on the ventilator. Should she have the right to refuse continued treatment?

That there can be good reason to refuse treatment is not a new idea. Treatment that is useless simply violates the principle of nonmaleficence. But what of treatment that might prolong life but exacts too high a price—be it physical, emotional, or financial? The Roman Catholic church grappled with this issue to help people determine when refusal of treatment is not a form of suicide but rather an appropriate moral choice. The theological underpinnings lie in the principle of double effect, first sketched by Saint Thomas Aquinas to justify killing in self-defense. Double effect arises from an action that one knows will produce both a good consequence and a bad consequence. The principle permits that act as long as four conditions can be met: The act itself must be good or at least neutral; the agent intends directly the act's good effect and only permits the evil effect; the good effect must not come about as a result of the evil effect; the situation must be sufficiently serious to warrant the permission of an evil effect. A classic example of justification based on double effect is the physician faced with a patient in severe pain. The principle of double effect allows the administration of medication to relieve pain even if it might also bring on death.

To apply the principle of double effect in the medical context, the church drew a distinction between ordinary care and extraordinary care. From their perspective, ordinary care offers a real possibility for benefit. Further, it is easily obtained and not excessively expensive. A patient should always accept ordinary care. By contrast, extraordinary care may be a gamble, with long odds for success. It may also entail unbearable pain, travel far from home, and formidable expense. There is no obligation to accept extraordinary care. All told, these considerations helped clarify the beneficence or nonmaleficence in a particular course of treatment.

Physicians have found the ordinary/extraordinary distinction a useful frame of reference, valuable for weighing treatment decisions. They often substitute customary/unusual for ordinary/extraordinary to describe standard medical practice. Thus Barney Clark, the first patient to try an artificial heart, may be said to have received extraordinary, or unusual, care. No one is morally required to pursue such heroic measures. Clark's case illuminates one of the problems with the ordinary/extraordinary distinction; the very nature of biomedicine makes the terms as changeable as a chameleon. If the artificial heart can be made to work, and work well, it will someday be standard medical practice and, as such, ordinary, or customary, care.

Ethicists tend to see the ordinary/extraordinary distinction in a larger context: that of the whole person with both a medical condition and a personal condition. Medical decisions are not purely medical but human, too. Our quandary is knowing when treatment is beneficent. That quandary is reshaped by each gain in medical science. But it is also reshaped by each individual. Every one of us has developed an entirely personal set of values by which we live our lives. Some of us can tolerate more pain than others. Some of us can overcome limitations that others find insuperable. Some of us can extract meaning and joy from circumstances too diminished for others. In short, if quality of life is considered, there is no single standard for beneficence; what is beneficent for one is not beneficent for all.

Applying the ordinary/extraordinary distinction is not always easy. The principle of nonmaleficence, requiring that the physician not hurt the patient, is violated—properly— every day. We endure the passing discomfort of an inoculation for the long-term benefit of protection from a disease that might permanently disable or kill us.

Consider Dax Cowart. Severely burned in a propane-gas explosion, he fought against treatment, which lasted for more than a year, from beginning to end. At the accident scene he begged to use a passerby's gun to commit suicide. He implored ambulance attendants to let him die. A plan to commit suicide by throwing himself out of his hospital room's window was foiled. Treatment required the removal of an eye and several fingers, and horrifically painful treatment for the burns. Cowart said, "It doesn't take a genius to know that when you're in that amount of pain, you can either bear it or you can't. And I couldn't."[4]

But he did. Now, nearly two decades later, Cowart has a law degree, a marriage, a full life. He is nonetheless still furious that he was allowed no role in the decision making about his treatment. Was his care ordinary or extraordinary? In medical terms it was ordinary, but in personal terms—at least, in Cowart's personal terms—it was extraordinary.

When a patient is looked at as a whole person, the issue of quality of life easily creeps into considerations about ordinary and extraordinary care. This may be problematic. Paul Ramsey, for example, asserts that quality-of-life considerations warp treatment decisions. He holds that the principle of autonomy, whereby a competent patient can refuse treatment, has been overdrawn: "There are medically indicated treatments . . . that a competent conscious patient has no moral right to refuse."[5]

Moreover, Ramsey believes that quality of life has gained outsize power, especially when applied to incompetent patients.

Quality-of-life considerations shift the question from whether "treatments are in some measure beneficial to patients to . . . whether patients' lives are beneficial to them."[6] To support his point, he cites the case of Joseph Saikewicz (see p. 8). References to quality of life in the court decisions struck Ramsey as proof that Saikewicz was not treated because of his retardation. Ordinary care would have called for chemotherapy for Saikewicz, just as it did for every other patient with the same diagnosis.

Discerning when treatment is ordinary because it is benefiting the patient is not an easy task. At a certain point, prolonging life gives way to prolonging the dying process. There is general agreement that the principle of beneficence is violated when treatment merely prolongs the dying process. But sensing just when dying has begun is extremely subjective.

This is true of physicians, too, despite—and because of—their training. The profession's tradition of battling disease and death often impels physicians to use any and every available therapy, even when by any reasonable standard none will cure. This is the technological imperative—technology's demand that if it is available, it must be used. The problem has become acute, and will grow even more so, because of the technologies that cannot always heal but often do sustain life. Jessica Muller and Barbara Koenig hold that "the orientation towards 'hope' influences physicians' actions in two ways: it encourages a treatment focus on whatever medical interventions are necessary to forestall death and, in the process, it allows physicians to delay the identification of patients as dying until death is unavoidable."[7] Indeed, they found that many physicians do not acknowledge that a patient is dying until "death is imminent or, in some cases, has already occurred."[8] Such situations are ineffably sad. Fiercely, finely committed to their patients' well-being, physicians who cannot accept death are unable to give the dying the very different, very essential kind of care that they need.

What is to be done when everyone agrees that treatment is only prolonging the dying process? Vitalists believe that you must still carry on with treatment. Otherwise, you kill as surely as if you put a gun to the patient's head and pull the trigger. They rail at Do Not Resuscitate orders, by which, for example, a patient in the last stages of terminal cancer is not revived in the event of cardiac arrest.

The majority of physicians and ethicists believe that there is a real difference between allowing to die and killing. The line is commonly drawn by using the distinction between acts of omission and acts of commission. The physician may not cause death by an act of commission—for example, by giving a patient a lethal injection. That is killing. But death that comes from an act of omission—for example, by withdrawing futile treatment—is proper. The physician is only allowing death, a result of disease, to occur. The distinction has its shaky side—withholding an insulin shot from a diabetic is an act of omission that does cause harm.[9]

Even those who are comfortable with the distinction between acts of omission and acts of commission acknowledge that it is very hard to stop treatment. Ending treatment, however useless, means giving up control. Giving up control, difficult in itself, is especially difficult for physicians. It is done in the face of failure, which some physicians are apt to internalize; they often regard a patient's death as the failure of their medical skill, not the inevitable failure of the human body.

To some, withdrawing even useless treatment is still an act of commission. They believe that the way to avoid the moral discomfort that comes with withdrawing treatment is to withhold treatment in the first place. Taking that tack would be disastrous, especially for accident victims. Aggressive treatment really works for many people who on first sight seem unsavable. If withholding treatment became the norm, undertreatment, not overtreatment, would become the rule.

Moral discomfort with the idea of withdrawing treatment is not the only problem. Groping to understand the implications of withdrawing treatment, our society has yet to agree on what treatment policies embody respect for life—and respect for death, too. The histories of ethics, medicine, and law are firmly based on the value of supporting life. Even when everyone agrees that treatment is useless, physicians and hospital administrators, fearful of criminal charges, often require court orders before allowing treatment to be withdrawn. The successes of biomedicine have brought us face to face with patients and families who insist that the right to die be recognized.

Such was the case of Karen Ann Quinlan. In the early morning hours of 15 April 1975 Quinlan was found blue and pulseless after attending a party where she had been drinking and perhaps taking tranquilizers. She was breathing at the hospital, but with some difficulty, so she was put on a ventilator to prevent further brain damage while a diagnosis was being made. It was soon clear that Quinlan was very ill. Within days of hospitalization, her body began drawing up into a fetal position.

Journalist Andrew Malcolm describes her family's response:

> The mother was first to see, as mothers often are with sick children. "You know," Julie Quinlan told her husband, "Karen's not going to make it."

"Don't you ever say that again!" he shot back. So she didn't. And she told their other children, Mary Ellen and John, not to say that either. It was another month before Joe Quinlan made the same announcement, and found his family nodding.[10]

Recognizing that Karen's condition was unchanged and that there was no reasonable hope for her recovery, they asked that the ventilator be disconnected and Karen be allowed to die. The hospital refused on the grounds that Karen was incompetent to make such a decision and that her parents could not make the decision on her behalf, and the court agreed. This struck her father as inconsistent: " 'The hospital needed my permission to begin her treatment,' Joe Quinlan said. 'But when I wanted to take her off, my word wasn't good enough.' "[11]

The case was appealed to the New Jersey Supreme Court, which reversed the lower court decision. It ruled that the Constitution's protection of a right to privacy allows a patient to refuse medical treatment; a guardian has the right to refuse treatment on behalf of an incompetent patient by the doctrine of substituted judgment, whereby the guardian decides what the patient would want if he or she were competent.

Quinlan's ventilator was turned off, but she did not die. Nourished by means of a feeding tube, Quinlan remained in her deep coma until her death in June 1985, more than nine years after the New Jersey Supreme Court agreed with her parents' claim that Karen Quinlan had a right to die.

Quinlan's case, dealing with substituted judgment, was also about the technological imperative. More and more the public began to wonder aloud whether medical technology is often applied indiscriminately. It seemed that our illusions about the capacities of biomedicine had clouded our thinking.

Before the twentieth century the goals of medicine were the provision of health, if possible, and care, always. Now medicine's goal was the prolongation of life. We sometimes forget that life itself is not the ultimate objective. Simply being alive permits but does not ensure all that makes life meaningful— experiencing, learning, participating, giving expression to the self. Bodily life is not all of life. Quinlan was alive, but she had lost her life.

The instinct for life and the fear of death are very powerful. Still, the worry about being overtreated is so potent that, beginning with California in 1976, states began passing legislation allowing for living wills. These are legal instruments by which competent adults can specify the circumstances under which life-sustaining treatment should be withdrawn if they become incompetent.

Some physicians opposed such legislation. It suggested that they could not be trusted to use their skills appropriately, or that withdrawing useless treatment was not already a part of accepted medical practice. Indeed, according to the American Hospital Association, treatment in one form or another is withdrawn from about 70 percent of the patients who die in hospitals.[12] Living wills are still criticized on the grounds that they could *require* life-sustaining technology. Might physicians be forced to give extraordinary care to patients who had not signed living wills?

The criteria for determining brain death pertain to patients with total brain death: Both the cortex, which governs thinking and feeling, and the brain stem, which governs all of the involuntary processes of the body, are completely inactive. Patients in what is called a persistent vegetative state, or PVS, are not brain dead. They have lost all cortical brain function, but the brain stem continues to function. Feeding via tubes placed through the nose or stomach wall is needed, but the heart and circulatory system continue to function on their own because the brain stem continues to function.

Those who caution that tinkering with the definition of death has eroded our reverence for life point to the case of Nancy Cruzan. On 11 January 1982 Cruzan's car skidded on ice and rolled several times before coming to rest in a muddy field in Missouri. Thrown from the car, Cruzan was found lying face down in the field; she had no heartbeat or pulse. Medics got her heart going and rushed her to the hospital, where she was stabilized.

Like Quinlan, Cruzan was in a persistent vegetative state. When they lost hope that she would ever emerge, Joe and Joyce Cruzan sought permission to exercise their daughter's right to die. They asked that the feeding tube surgically implanted in her stomach, the one bit of technology keeping her body going, be removed.

If a feeding tube is removed, the patient will die of starvation, and this makes many quail. "For willful starvation there can be no excuse," the philosopher G. E. M. Anscombe has declared.[13] Laden with nutrients, food is also laden with the powerful symbolism of people caring for people. Indeed, when it was suggested that Karen Quinlan be taken off the feeding tube, as well as the ventilator, her father was shocked: "Oh no," Joseph Quinlan protested. "That is her nourishment."[14] To deny food, many hold, is as cruel and inhumane as to deny a patient a blanket. Food is a form of basic care, not a cure. Even the perfectly healthy need it every day. When we sit down to a meal, we do not sit down for a medical treatment.

But are artificial nutrition and hydration just basic care? A feeding tube is every bit as artificial a way to provide nutrients as a ventilator is to provide oxygen. Many who agree that Cruzan had a right to die maintain that she was to all intents and purposes already dead. Dehydration and starvation can be extremely painful, but Cruzan could not feel pain.

Karen Quinlan and Nancy Cruzan were caught up in a formal debate about the use of life-support systems when cure proves impossible. Equally important, their cases raised the question of treatment decisions for incompetents. The concept of substituted judgment is fiercely attacked because it depends on leaps of logic. A competent patient can claim a right to die and support it with the principle of autonomy. An incompetent patient has lost his or her autonomy. Many believe that autonomy cannot be transferred to and exercised by another. Those who oppose substituted judgment say that the concept is not only illogical but also soft: There is no way to ensure that a guardian does anything more than choose what the guardian wants done for the patient. Vitalists dismiss the idea of substituted judgment as nothing more than a ploy to let a guardian wriggle free of richly deserved guilt; allowing a patient to die is in fact a euphemism for killing that patient.

Missouri law allowed termination of treatment for patients who had formally made their views known. Cruzan, who was twenty-five at the time of her accident, had not signed a living will. But she had at various times expressed her opinion that she would not want to live unless she could do so "halfway normally."[15] A Missouri lower court accepted these statements, but the state's supreme court deemed them "unreliable."[16] The Cruzans took their case to the U.S. Supreme Court, which heard arguments on 6 December 1989.

James Bopp, Jr., president of the National Legal Center for the Medically Dependent and Disabled, assailed the Cruzans' claim for their right to exercise patient autonomy on Nancy's behalf:

Informed consent requires: that the patient have a capacity to reason and make judgments; and that there be a clear understanding of the nature of the disease and its prognosis. Since, under the hypothetical circumstances, neither the benefits nor the risks of treatment can be properly weighed, any statements Nancy made prior to her automobile accident regarding life-sustaining treatment did not constitute informed refusal of care.[17]

Bopp then rebutted the argument that artificial nutrition and hydration are simply medical treatments:

A quality of life assessment is implicit when recovery is adopted as the standard to determine when food and fluids should be provided a patient. Food and fluids only maintain life; they do not treat an illness or restore brain cells. Thus the claim that because Nancy will not recover she should not be fed "is but a thinly disguised statement that her life in its present form is not worth living." Using "recovery" as a standard shifts the issue from whether treatments are beneficial to the patient to whether patients' lives are beneficial to them.[18]

Not having signed a living will was a big problem for Cruzan. But having signed a living will might still have been a big problem—keep in mind Bopp's view that "any statements Nancy made prior to her automobile accident regarding life-sustaining treatment did not constitute informed refusal of care."

Those who accept living wills accept their vagueness, too. As Susan Wolf observes:

It is true that Nancy did not enumerate treatment modalities. It is also true that Nancy did not name the precise condition she would later be in, though "vegetable" in lay terms comes awfully close. But people trying to express their preferences about how they wish to die cannot be expected to go down a laundry list of treatment modalities and have a fit of clairvoyance in which they correctly name the condition that will later overtake them.[19]

So stark was Cruzan's condition that life, not quality of life, is the issue in her case and in the cases of the estimated ten thousand other Americans who lie in the same persistent vegetative state.[20] But what of the thousands upon thousands of Americans who are in an equally hopeless but less extreme condition?

In June 1990 the U.S. Supreme Court handed down its decision in the Cruzan case. The justices held that there is a right to die, and they deemed artificial nutrition and hydration a medical treatment. They held, however, that the state of Missouri had a right to set its own requirements for clear and convincing evidence that the patient would want treatment ended. The court would not order that the feeding tube be removed.

Later that year the Cruzans went back to court with new testimony supporting their contention that Nancy would not want to live as she was. Her court-appointed guardian, Thad C. McCanse, observed, "There comes a time when litigation must be ended, when difficult questions must be resolved and when reason should triumph over ritual."[21] The new testimony was accepted, the feeding tube was removed, and Cruzan died twelve days later.

Was her care mere ritual? Was her death beneficent? Was she allowed to die, or was she killed?

Euthanasia, a word derived from Thanatos, the Greek personification of death, means "good death." From ancient times on, a good death has been understood as a death without suffering. In the twentieth century, however, the term euthanasia has come to include mercy killing, usually by a lethal injection. This is sometimes referred to as active euthanasia to distinguish it from the withdrawal of medical treatment. In its narrowest sense, active euthanasia means causing the death of someone who is already close to death and in severe, intractable pain. More rarely, active euthanasia is proposed for patients like Nancy Cruzan. Yet Cruzan was not terminally ill—physicians maintained that she could live another thirty years as long as nutrition and hydration were provided—and she was not in pain.

To redress what some saw as an imbalance between the principles of beneficence and nonmaleficence, the British Voluntary Euthanasia Society and the Euthanasia Society of America were founded in the 1930s. The timing tells much of the story. As medicine as a science took hold, the nature of death changed. Increasingly, people died not after a short joust with infectious disease but after a long—and often painful—competition with chronic illness. Biomedicine's darker side is its paradoxical power to keep the patient alive but still suffering.

The British society quickly presented a proposal to legalize voluntary active euthanasia—mercy killing at the request of the patient—but it was defeated in the House of Lords in 1936 by a vote of thirty-five to fourteen. Then World War II intervened and provided a view of involuntary euthanasia—the killing of the ill without their consent—in its most corrupted form. During the 1920s and 1930s, German medical and legal literature explored ideas of *lebensunwerten*

Leben—"life not worthy of life." The Nazis translated that concept into a program of murder tricked out as euthanasia. Beginning in 1939 with the severely or chronically ill, then adding those mentally and physically handicapped who were deemed socially unproductive, the regime quietly did away with some one hundred thousand Aryan Germans.[22] They were supposedly taken to clinics, where they supposedly died of heart attacks, the flu, or the like. The program slowed down in 1941 only because of growing public protest as Germans began to put together what was happening. The cat was out of the bag.

The German "euthanasia" program was a powerful setback to those who believed active euthanasia should be legal. If such a vile program could be instituted in Germany, a nation that laid heavy emphasis on education and culture, what was to prevent it from being instituted in Britain or the United States?

But euthanasia has proved an insistent idea, retaining its currency because the new medical technology continues to deliver many patients to a seemingly intolerable netherworld between life and death. Despite the fact that active euthanasia is illegal, people have increasingly said the law be damned and have killed family members they believed would want to be dead. Andrew Malcolm offers a telling anecdote:

> . . . I remember reading a newspaper item about an old man in Texas with a wife long-stricken with Alzheimer's disease. He had walked into his wife's hospital room one day, shot her dead and turned the pistol on himself. A few weeks later, haunted by this freakish incident, I called the hospital spokesman. I said I wanted to talk about the old man who had killed his chronically ill wife. And the spokesman said to me, "Which one?"[23]

That the public sympathizes with people caught up in such situations seems to be borne out by the legal disposition of twenty-nine mercy-killing cases between 1980 and 1985:

- 2 refusals to indict
- 1 dismissal
- 2 acquittals
- 1 not guilty verdict by reason of temporary insanity
- 21 manslaughter convictions with suspended sentence or probation
- 2 murder convictions with imprisonment[24]

Those who oppose legalizing active euthanasia place the emphasis on killing. Pointing to the Nazi program, they hold that once the prohibition against killing is loosened, there is no way that it can be stopped. They argue that the way to handle these desperate cases is not to legalize euthanasia. Instead, we must provide the care the terminally ill and their care givers need.

Critics looking at active euthanasia from a theological point of view say it goes against God's law. We are merely stewards of our lives; it is for God to decide when our lives are to end. Further, suffering is an inevitable part of life; our task is to understand and grow from suffering, not evade it.

Active euthanasia is also criticized on medical grounds. Diagnosis can be wrong. Furthermore, a cure for what is today incurable might be found tomorrow. And what of informed consent? Can a patient struggling with pain and the enormity of death make a truly rational decision to end his or her life? Consider the case of one patient with kidney disease who asked to be taken off dialysis and be allowed to die. Pursuing the question right after a dialysis, the physician asked if the patient indeed wanted to stop treatment. "Don't listen to me," the patient replied. "That's my uremia talking, not me. I want to stay in the program."[25]

Finally, active euthanasia is criticized because of what it will do to the physician-patient relationship across the board. Medicine has a long and venerable tradition. Every profession has its scoundrels, but by and large physicians throughout the ages have demonstrated a passionate commitment to relieve suffering and maximize the body's functioning. We depend on physicians not simply because, lacking their expertise, we must. We depend on physicians because we trust them. As ethicist James Childress observes:

> The distinction between killing and letting die is so interwoven with our understanding of medical care that we cannot remove it without tearing the whole fabric. To authorize physicians to kill patients would so alter the ethos of medicine that a new basis for trust would be necessary.[26]

Those who favor legalizing active euthanasia place the emphasis on mercy. They begin by asserting that the Nazi example is a red herring. It was conceived to serve the interests of the Nazi regime, not the interests of the individual, and it was carried out not at the request or with the consent of the patient.

Proponents of active euthanasia counter the theological arguments in two ways. They note that stewardship has not prevented the religious from exercising control in other areas of their lives—for example, in using analgesics for surgery and childbirth. If it is for God to decide when life will end, if suffering is ennobling, then the very practice of medicine is and always has been wrong. Further, they hold that theological arguments against active euthanasia pertain only to the religious; the constitutional separation of church and state requires that opposition to active euthanasia on theological grounds alone not be codified in law.

In our increasingly secular society, many believe that humans are sovereigns, not stewards, of their own lives. For them, it follows that respect for autonomy should mean respect for a person's decision to end his or her life. How can we demand that someone endure unbearable pain just so that we can be morally comfortable? Palliation, the control of pain, is a relatively young medical specialty. Its practitioners have only begun to explore therapies, drugs, and the manner and timing of drug administration to maximize effectiveness and minimize side effects. Forcing a person to endure a degrading and dispiriting bondage to unremitting pain is cruel. And, say proponents of active euthanasia, it dishonors the principle of the sanctity of life. "Ending the life of a person who wants it ended because of unsupportable agony is the very opposite of indifference to life,"[27] asserts ethicist Daniel Maguire.

Some maintain that to speak of allowing the patient to die and forgoing life-sustaining treatment is to speak of passive euthanasia. If some cases call for nonmaleficence in the form of passive euthanasia, other cases call for beneficence in the form of active euthanasia. Diagnoses can be wrong, but for the most part they are very accurate, especially when disease is so far advanced that euthanasia is discussed. At that stage death will not be held off even if a miracle cure is found. Proponents of legalizing active euthanasia respect the trust that springs from the physician-patient relationship. But they feel sure that that essential trust can be protected by establishing tight procedures to ensure that active euthanasia is not abused.

Emily Bauer, who expressed in plain terms the fear of dying so many share, ultimately chose active euthanasia. The thought of dying if an attendant was not present when her ventilator accidently slipped loose filled her with dread. But the disease, which had rendered her unable to move a muscle, even her tongue, made her long for death. Arrangements were made for a day trip home from the hospital. There a physician came and gave her a lethal injection.

For Bauer, life had become unbearably useless. What primarily fires the euthanasia movement is life that has become unbearably painful. Elizabeth Latimer, a physician who specializes in palliative care at Hamilton Civic Hospitals in Canada, deals with many people who are dying. By her estimate, pain cannot be significantly controlled in 15 to 20 percent of the cases. Especially interesting, though, is her observation that of the more than three thousand patients she has cared for since 1982, she can count on one hand those who broached the subject of euthanasia.[28]

What, then, makes euthanasia such a compelling issue? That it resonates at such a deep level in the healthy but not in the dying must give us pause; that discrepancy suggests that much of the intellectual and emotional terrain of euthanasia remains uncharted. Helplessly watching someone in severe pain has its own very real, very anguishing pain. Perhaps the healthy unconsciously confuse the release of a loved one from physical pain with their own release from emotional pain.

Voluntary active euthanasia, in which a person asks that death be brought on, is a form of suicide. What generally distinguishes euthanasia from suicide is the imminence of death and the dependence on the aid of a physician. Like euthanasia, suicide figures prominently in bioethics today. Each year in the United States about twenty-eight thousand deaths are certified as suicides, although some deaths classified as accidents are no doubt suicides.[29] How inaccurate the figures are is not clear. What is clear is that suicides are rising, particularly among teenagers. Suicide intrigues us on one level or another. Derek Humphry's *Final Exit,* a manual on how to commit suicide published in 1991, found a place on the best-seller list.

Just as intrigued were ancient Greek philosophers, who were divided on the subject. Some, like the Stoics, approved of suicide. As long as it was a rational rather than desperate act, suicide reflected human integrity and dignity. Aristotelians disapproved on the grounds that it robbed the state of a person who was its property.

Suicide was common among the early Christians. Eager for the hereafter, fearful that earthly temptations would make them sin, thereby jeopardizing their entry into heaven, many turned to suicide. The epidemic of suicide was stemmed only when Saint Augustine pronounced suicide a grave sin, graver than any that could be committed on earth. From then on, church law was shaped to discourage the practice. People who had committed suicide could not be given burial rites, and those who attempted suicide but failed were excommunicated. As secular law developed, it too supported church teaching. A suicide's property was confiscated and the family dishonored. But the harshness of those laws was such that by the eighteenth century, they had fallen into disuse.

The view of suicide as a sin has given way to the view of suicide as a mental-health problem. Life presents many difficulties. When they pile up, finding even one refuge in life to retreat to can seem impossible. Overwhelmed, one is robbed of the ability to see ways to handle the difficulties. No one in such a state can make a rational decision about life. With that shift, compassion dictated that suicide be decriminalized. At the same time, the principle of beneficence dictated that every effort be made to intervene in someone's effort to commit suicide and get that person much-needed help.

"In any context," David Smith observes, "suicide is a social act, the unanswerable gesture in a social dialogue."[30] For this reason morality has traditionally demanded that we do what we can to stop the individual from a rash act. Suicide intervention serves to keep the social dialogue going long enough for a person's instinct for life to rebound. But this form of beneficence is now being challenged by rising claims for the individual's right to autonomy. In an effort to mediate between these conflicting principles, Thomas Szasz distinguishes between suicide and attempted suicide, each of which, he believes, means something different: "Generally speaking, the person who commits suicide intends to die; whereas the one who threatens suicide or makes an unsuccessful attempt at it intends to improve his life, not terminate it."[31]

Szasz's distinction between attempted suicide and suicide may be too neat. Nonetheless, many agree with his premise that intervention in a person's efforts to end life is an attack on human dignity. They maintain that one can be perfectly sane and find that the conditions necessary for a worthwhile life are beyond one's grasp. Suicide prevention can be simply a heavy-handed short-circuiting of autonomy.

That is how Janet Adkins saw it. At fifty-four she was coping with the early stages of Alzheimer's disease. Knowing the inevitable horror of advanced Alzheimer's, she decided she wanted no part of it. In June 1990 she flew from her home in Oregon to Michigan, where she hoped to be the first to use Dr. Jack Kevorkian's suicide machine. Kevorkian would hook her up to an intravenous tube by which saline solution flowed into her body. When she pushed a button, thiopental, then potassium chloride, would be released, causing a painless death within minutes. All went according to plan.

The case drew national attention, in large measure because of the circumstances surrounding Adkins's suicide. An ardent advocate of assisted suicide, Kevorkian was not in the position to weigh what was best for Adkins; because her death would serve to advance his cause, his advice was suspect. Kevorkian, a pathologist with no specialized background in Alzheimer's disease, evaluated Adkins in the course of a dinner conversation. The next day Kevorkian put his machine and a cot in an old van, and he and Adkins drove to a park for her death.

Murray Raskind, Adkins's physician, contended that she could have expected three or four more years of good life before the severe dementia that characterizes Alzheimer's disease took hold. Still, he maintained that her judgment had been impaired enough to make her incompetent to make the decision to end her life. Geoffrey Fieger, Kevorkian's lawyer, retorted: "If she had such a great life ahead of her, how was she mentally incompetent?"[32]

Kevorkian's assistance in suicide is not uncommon, though physicians themselves have no idea how often their colleagues help their patients in this way. In March 1991 Timothy Quill published an article describing his involvement in the suicide of one of his patients, a forty-five-year-old woman he called Diane. Having refused treatment for acute leukemia because the treatment is especially rigorous and would offer only a 25 percent chance of cure, she began exploring the question of suicide with Quill. He referred her to the Hemlock Society, a national organization that strongly supports the right to die. When Diane called Quill for a prescription for a barbiturate for sleep, Quill recognized the request for what it was: The Hemlock Society recommends it as a method of suicide. Quill gave her the prescription and told her the dosage for sleep, the dosage for suicide. Diane chose suicide.

Following publication of Quill's article, the district attorney sent the case to a grand jury, which refused to indict him. From the start, many ethicists believed Quill had acted in a highly ethical fashion. Unlike Kevorkian, Quill had known his patient for eight years. Quill, Diane, and Diane's family had explored the question thoughtfully and thoroughly. Quill had required Diane to discuss her situation with a psychologist, who agreed that she was competent to make the decision to end her life. Only then did Quill prescribe the drug.[33]

Slowly, surely, we are as individuals and as a society exploring the right to die. Those who see the right to die as not enough, who want real and total control, demand that we explore active euthanasia and suicide as well. How will we come to terms with dying and death? Uneasily, endlessly.

BIOETHICS AT THE
BEGINNING OF LIFE

Another arena in which the problematic nature of the term *quality of life* is seen is the neonatal intensive care unit. Neonatology—the care of newborns at risk—is a young specialty, dating from the 1960s. It originally focused its efforts on premature infants and on full-term but low-birth-weight infants. Now the extraordinary mobilization of medical technology has enabled some newborns weighing as little as a loaf of bread—five hundred grams, or just over one pound—to survive.

The more premature the infant, the higher the incidence of defects that can come with prematurity. Lung failure and bleeding in the brain are particularly common because the lungs and brain have not had sufficient time to develop. So as the specialty has developed, its practitioners have taken on infants with abnormalities that most certainly would have been fatal before, as well as full-term normal babies who were injured in the birth process. All told, neonatologists deal with about 6 percent of all infants born each year.[1] Aggressive treatment pulls some through a rocky period; discharged, they go home to grow up like any other normal child. Others go home handicapped, but those handicaps are very much lighter than they would have been without intensive, specialized care. On the other hand, some infants go to the neonatal intensive care unit to die. All-out efforts to save them would be to no avail, and the principle of nonmaleficence requires that they not be subjected to treatment that would provide only more suffering.

The bedeviling cases are those in which aggressive treatment cannot correct or significantly ameliorate the defects but might prolong the patients' lives. Before the advent of neonatology these children posed no ethical question; they could not, and did not, survive. Now, having the ability to save many of these children, we sometimes wonder if we always should try to save them. By outwitting natural selection, which favors the strongest, do we place an intolerable burden on these children? Is it beneficent to subject children with severe defects to possible unremitting pain—pain that is crueler still when the child has no intellectual basis for understanding it? Is it beneficent to lock those that survive into a life in which all their energy will be spent on dealing with their handicaps?

There is much talk about saving more and more infants, who are then condemned to a wretched existence in "dying bins." That perception, however, is off base. The number of children saved by aggressive treatment in neonatal intensive care units is indeed increasing. So, too, is the number of children who are freed of handicaps. As new technology comes into the practice of neonatology, children who only a few years ago might have merely survived can now often truly flourish. The success rate *is* climbing.

Nonetheless, it is often charged that many very ill newborns become victims of vitalism. Many argue that in doing everything imaginable to save their severely impaired patients, physicians subject them to sheer torture. Another, darker charge is that aggressive treatment for an infant is not always for that child's benefit. This criticism is often raised in connection with premature infants at the margin of viability—the point at which the fetus is able to survive outside of the womb. Aggressive treatment may or may not save them. Some accuse neonatologists of making such attempts for the sake of learning. In such cases the principle of beneficence is not at issue. The infant is used simply to extend the field of neonatology. Paul Ramsey asks, "Do you have to experiment on earlier and earlier neonates to make normal the ones we learned to save some years ago?"[2]

Robert Stinson believes that medical experimentation is a powerful force in neonatology. Using as an example the case of his son, he asserts that "the very object of treatment—beyond the care of infants—is to find out if there *are* any limits."[3] Andrew Stinson, born in December 1976, was about sixteen weeks premature. During the next week, his weight sank from eight hundred grams to six hundred. Transferred to a regional hospital that had a neonatal intensive care unit, he was aggressively treated. Treatment provided no clear benefits, other than sheer survival, but a multitude of iatrogenic conditions (that is, conditions caused by medical care itself) did emerge. At one point his bones, demineralized, began breaking spontaneously. Brain seizures, lung disorders, repeated infections, a heart defect, microcephaly (an abnormally small head size, which generally signals mental retardation)—these are but a few of the medical problems he faced.

The Stinsons wanted treatment stopped, but the physicians refused. "What they never understood," Robert Stinson laments, "was that one *can* care deeply enough about a child like Andrew to want his misery ended. Allowing Andrew to die naturally was what we wanted *for* him, not just to him."[4]

In 1976 Andrew's chances for survival were very, very slim. Now, in the early 1990s, close to 50 percent of the babies weighing 500 to 750 grams at birth survive. But of those that do survive, the majority have neurological damage.[5]

Physicians and ethicists generally agree that some handicapped newborns should not be treated. That is about all that they agree on. One debate focuses on which infants should be allowed to die. Some say that all handicapped newborns that are not obviously dying should be treated. Others maintain that nontreatment can be justified for newborns with handicaps that fall into a wide range of categories. Another debate focuses on who decides. Physicians? Parents? What reasons justify the decision not to treat them? Would the parents' unwillingness to take on the burden of a handicapped child justify a nontreatment decision? Ethical arguments have been advanced for positions from one end of the spectrum to the other. Indeed, some believe that infanticide—the killing of an infant—would be proper in some cases.

Consensus about which handicapped newborns to treat is lacking in part because of the difficulty in making a diagnosis. In some cases it is impossible to diagnose the nature and extent of a defect. What appears to be a defect is sometimes not a defect at all but rather a lag in development. Figuring out whether an abnormality is permanent and severe is often merely a guessing game when neonatologists start working on a patient.

Even if an accurate diagnosis can be made, an accurate prognosis might still be elusive. Neonatologists can quote statistics for outcomes in various kinds of cases, but they often cannot predict which infant will do well, which infant will do poorly. Further, because neonatologists are now saving children who only a few years ago would not have survived, there is little long-range information by which to evaluate the various new courses of treatment and their potential long-term benefit. For example, it is now being found that some children who seemed to escape the intellectual and physical impairments that can result from prematurity begin demonstrating learning disorders and behavioral problems when they start school.

Of all medical specialists, neonatologists agree least on what constitutes standard medical practice. Consider, for example, treatment for newborns with spina bifida. Spina bifida results when the neural tube, a sack that holds the nerves running up and down the spinal column, fails to form early on in a pregnancy. Because the tube is not completely closed, tissue and fluid can spill into the spinal column. More commonly, a lesion on the back causes tissue to be exposed and cerebrospinal fluid to leak. As a consequence the patient suffers some degree of paralysis in the legs. Skin sometimes forms naturally to close the wound on its own, but if it does not, the risk of infection is great. Infants do not die of spina bifida itself. They die of infection or of the other problems—notably heart disease—that often accompany the defect.

John Lorber, a pediatric surgeon in Sheffield, England, has changed his approach to spina bifida. At first he treated all of his patients aggressively, but after years of watching how they did, he turned to selective nontreatment as a way to save infants from needless suffering. He distinguishes between those patients who will benefit from care and those who will never have a meaningful life even if treated or who will probably die within a year if untreated.

The medical criteria he uses to determine which children to treat include the extent of paralysis, the severity of the wound, the extent of curvature of the spine, enlarged head, brain damage sustained at birth, and other possible birth defects, such as heart disease and Down's syndrome. Many patients fail to make the cut. In one twenty-one-month period, twenty-five out of thirty-seven newborns with spina bifida were not treated. Those left untreated died within nine months of birth. Of those who were treated, one died; the rest survived and are considered "normal or moderately handicapped."[6]

In contrast, Lorber's colleague R. B. Zachary treats nearly all comers. He does not perform surgery on infants with spina bifida who will surely die within a few days of birth. But those who have a lesion that surgery can close and who are not actually dying he treats—and quickly, at that. Surgery early on to close the lesion means less paralysis, as well as less opportunity for infection. Hydrocephalus controlled from the beginning means less retardation. Zachary maintains that infants who are not treated but unexpectedly survive are more handicapped than they would have been if surgery had been performed just after birth. So it is that he treats not to save lives but to save whatever capacity is there. Looking at two hundred cases over one ten-year period, Zachary considers 56 percent of them to have had a "reasonable result"[7] because of treatment, and he believes that the rate for those same children would now be much higher because of new ways to control infection.

As the approaches taken by these two physicians demonstrate, there is a staggering lack of uniformity in decisions about which infants will be treated and which infants will not be treated. The absence of any general standard reflects the difficulty in attempting to resolve quality-of-life questions.

Infants with Down's syndrome make for classic cases in which to discuss quality of life. Caused by an extra chromosome 21, it is therefore often referred to as trisomy 21. Those afflicted with Down's syndrome typically have IQs in the range of twenty-five to sixty, although some, less touched by retardation, have IQs in the eighties. Accompanying minor physical abnormalities include shortened fingers and slanting eyes with epicanthic folds—a feature that accounts for the use of the term *mongoloid,* a term that has been discarded in recent years because of its potential to stigmatize. Down's syndrome infants often have major abnormalities, too. About 40 percent have heart problems, and all are more susceptible to infection.[8]

Consider what has come to be known as the Johns Hopkins Hospital case. A child born in 1963 at the Johns Hopkins Hospital was diagnosed as having Down's syndrome. In addition, he had a duodenal atresia—a blockage of the intestine. The infant's parents, a nurse and a lawyer, had two older children, and they worried that the enormous burden of caring for and raising a child with Down's syndrome would deprive his siblings of advantages and the parental energy and attention that all children need. The parents refused to give permission to treat—surgery to correct the blockage would not be performed. And so for the next eleven days the infant slowly died of starvation and dehydration.

Parents' concern about raising a handicapped child in our society is very real and justified. Historically our society has made only grudging provision for the handicapped. Institutional care for those too handicapped to be cared for at home; rehabilitation to maximize mobility and comfort; educational programs specifically tailored to a handicapped child's needs, abilities, and potential—all are meager, uneven in quality, and expensive. Most of us do not have to wrestle with the constant problem of finding the services a child with permanent defects needs. Still, we must wrestle with our society's imbalances. If the principle of beneficence impels us to save hitherto unsavable infants, it should also impel us to provide what they need after discharge from a glossy neonatal intensive care unit.

Further, our society is changing in ways that make it increasingly hard to care for the handicapped. The extended family, with grandparents and aunts and uncles and cousins to lighten the burden by sharing the burden, is now a rarity. Even the nuclear family, with two adults to provide care, seems almost as endangered as the bald eagle. As our horizons broaden, we are often drawn away from the community where we were born. Now we move about, often a number of times. If we benefit by having the opportunity to change and custom-fit our lives, we often pay the price of losing a supportive community of friends and neighbors known for decades.

Employment possibilities are changing, too. Automation and technology call for a labor force more and more in command of advanced skills. Businesses are less and less able to accommodate the handicapped. Parents' fears that their handicapped child will enter an inhospitable world are understandable. If parents worry about their ability to raise a handicapped child now, imagine their worry about the future. In the 1940s life expectancy for a Down's syndrome baby was twelve years. Now, because of better living conditions and medical care, a Down's syndrome baby can be expected to live into his or her fifties.[9] The severely handicapped never achieve independence. Who will take on the responsibility to care for and love the handicapped when their parents grow old and eventually die?

Many ethicists believe that the decision to let the child born at the Johns Hopkins Hospital die was wrong.[10] They begin by arguing that the child was not in fact dying. Even in the 1960s surgery for atresias was relatively straightforward and had a good success rate. Further, the surgery does more than ameliorate the blockage; it *fixes* it. Those who believe the decision was wrong point out that it was governed not by medical need but by the fact that the infant had Down's syndrome; an otherwise normal infant born with an atresia would automatically have been given the surgery. Even trying to justify the decision by the presence of Down's syndrome is not satisfactory. The degree of retardation cannot be determined in infants. Many babies with Down's syndrome grow up to function very well.

Another Down's syndrome case, one involving a child with an atresia—this time of the esophagus—along with an opening between the trachea and esophagus, came up in April 1982 in Bloomington, Indiana. Different neonatologists offered different odds for surgery: Some estimated an 85 to 90 percent chance of success, while others estimated a 50–50 chance of success. When the parents decided against surgery, the hospital sought a court order to require treatment. The lower court refused to order surgery, and the Indiana Supreme Court declined to review that decision. County prosecutors were trying to get the U.S. Supreme Court to intervene when "Infant Doe" died of starvation at the age of six days.[11]

The child's death did not put the matter to rest. A month later, at President Reagan's behest, the Department of Health and Human Services notified all hospitals that withholding food or medical treatment from a handicapped infant simply because the child is handicapped would be in violation of Section 504 of the Rehabilitation Act of 1973. Hospitals in violation of these so-called Baby Doe rules could lose their federal funds. On 2 March 1983 a zinger was added: The rules were amended to require the conspicuous posting of signs in hospital obstetric and pediatric units saying

DISCRIMINATORY FAILURE TO FEED AND CARE FOR
HANDICAPPED INFANTS IN THIS FACILITY IS PROHIBITED
BY FEDERAL LAW. FAILURE TO FEED AND CARE FOR INFANTS
MAY ALSO VIOLATE THE CRIMINAL AND CIVIL LAWS
OF YOUR STATE.

An 800 number was set up for lodging anonymous complaints.

The rules were challenged by the American Academy of Pediatrics and soon after were invalidated by Judge Gerhard Gesell. On 5 July 1983 the Department of Health and Human Services issued new Baby Doe rules redesigned so as to pass judicial scrutiny. They were softened by a statement that the department had never intended to force physicians to attempt treatment in futile cases. Still, their purpose was to limit the sphere of decision making in which physicians and parents move. Six months later these revised regulations were also invalidated by the courts on technical grounds. The Baby Doe rules, the court held, could not be piggybacked on the Rehabilitation Act of 1973, which was drafted to ensure the handicapped equal access to jobs, housing, and the like.

In response, amendments to the Child Abuse Prevention and Treatment Act were passed and signed into law by Ronald Reagan on 9 October 1984. The amendments make it illegal to withhold treatment unless the infant is comatose, treatment will only prolong dying, or treatment will be futile or inhumane. To what extent these rules would hold up if challenged in court is not known. Lawrence Nelson, asserting that they are "not as potent as one would think,"[12] believes that they have nonetheless hurt the practice of neonatology. Unclear about the law, unwilling to tangle with the law, physicians tend to overtreat their young patients. The result, according to Nelson, is infants forced to suffer more than they should suffer and parents actively excluded from the decision-making process. Meanwhile, the law has netted few cases of abuse. In just under three years after taking effect, only nineteen complaints were filed nationwide; of those, only six were acted on.[13]

The courts, of course, are called upon—properly so—when treatment decisions seem out of bounds, but they cannot be expected to solve all the problems. To begin, not all cases are acted on. Prosecutors learn of such cases only when someone, privy to and upset with a nontreatment decision, informs the authorities. If prosecutors do learn of a case, they often forgo filing charges. It is generally agreed that the state should not intervene in cases for which there is no proven treatment for the defect, where physicians disagree about the best course of treatment, or in which a proposed treatment has only a slim chance of success. Further, the complexity of medical science and the traditional respect for the role of physicians and parents in treatment decisions makes prosecutors sometimes reluctant to pursue cases that might be appropriate for legal intervention.

Cases that do go to court are decided with the same lack of uniformity that characterizes decisions made within hospitals. The court in the Bloomington, Indiana, Infant Doe case supported the parents' right to make a decision. And that child had fewer problems than the son born to Lorraine and Robert Houle in 1974. Parts of his left side were malformed: He had no left eye, only part of a left ear, a malformed left hand. Air moved into his stomach, while fluids from his stomach moved into his lungs. A fistula—or opening—between the trachea and the esophagus necessitated intravenous feeding. Brain damage was also suspected. Parlous even at birth, the infant's condition worsened in the days just after. Pneumonia took hold, and his reflexes deteriorated.

Physicians determined that surgery could correct the fistula, but given all of his other problems, the parents refused to give their consent for it. Some of the physicians disagreed with the decision and set in motion a neglect suit. In this case, the judge ordered surgery, which was performed, but the infant died the next day.[14]

In another difficult case, Siamese twins, weighing nine pounds, twelve ounces at birth, were born to Pam and Robert Mueller in 1981. On first seeing the boys, joined just below the waist and sharing three legs between them, the obstetrician decided to leave them to die in the delivery room—a decision the father agreed with. But the boys began breathing spontaneously, so they were taken to the nursery, there to be given no food or water.

An anonymous telephone call to the Illinois Department of Children and Family Services brought an investigation, then neglect charges against the parents. The department was given temporary custody of the children, who were sent to a neonatal intensive care unit in another hospital for treatment. Criminal charges against the parents and attending physician were filed, but at the preliminary hearing, none of the nurses who were called to testify could or would implicate the parents or obstetrician, so the charges were dismissed. When they were just over four months old, the boys were returned to their parents' custody.[15]

Although any court action might well be unlikely, the range of decisions that have been handed down in the few cases that have gone to court makes legal action a potential wild card in treatment decisions. Half of the neonatologists polled in a 1988 survey said that they had overtreated patients to protect themselves from prosecution.[16] With no clear trail blazed, overtreatment appears to have become standard medical practice in neonatology.

Some, however, welcomed the Baby Doe rules, believing that decisions about nontreatment of handicapped infants fell on a spectrum far too broad to be acceptable. They hold that nontreatment decisions should be made on the basis of medical classification rather than on an individual basis. How can we square herculean efforts to save one severely handicapped infant with nontreatment for the mildly handicapped infant in the next crib?

Those who believe the Baby Doe rules are appropriate recognize the parents' devastation and disappointment on finding that their eagerly awaited child is handicapped. Still, they point out, we have only to look around us to see handicapped people not only coping with their handicaps but also leading meaningful, happy lives. Pinning so much importance on intelligence, we forget all the other facets of life that give it purpose, depth, and joy. Birth represents entry into the community. The infant is a member of a family, a society, the human species. When we decide that a handicapped infant should die, we do violence to the community, as well as to that child. If we refuse to honor the child's legitimate claims to our care and protection, can we be assured that our own legitimate claims to care and protection will be honored?

However, even those who saw a need for government intervention often agree that the Baby Doe regulations were both in themselves and in the manner of their promulgation unfortunate. To begin, they are vague. Further, they reflect simplistic views of neonatology's tiny, often mysterious patients. First drafted with the Bloomington Down's syndrome case in mind, the regulations do not reflect the number and variety of defects or the differences in severity even within a single class of defects. The Department of Health and Human Services's failure to consult with physicians and hospital staffs, its brash effort to tie its regulations to legislation that addressed other issues, and its setting up of an 800 number seemed an arrogant and needlessly confrontational response to the problems of nontreatment decisions. The regulations implied that honorable, genuinely caring physicians and parents are the exception rather than the rule.

In fact, American neonatologists take a more vitalist approach than do their counterparts in other countries. Nancy Rhoden found that Swedish and British neonatologists make their treatment decisions on the basis of rather different goals. The Swedish policy

> does not regard the death of an individual infant who could have been saved as the worst type of error. . . . This strategy instead seeks to minimize the number of infants who die slow deaths or who live with profound handicaps, and is willing to sacrifice some potentially "good" survivors to achieve this goal.[17]

The British policy uses what Rhoden calls the individualized prognostic strategy. It is a moderate approach that does not depend on strict adherence to arbitrary medical classifications. This

> avoids the extremes of either treating all infants until the outcome is certain [the policy in the U.S.] or withholding treatment because the infant is in a class whose prognosis is grim [the policy in Sweden]. Neither type of mistake— sacrificing a potentially "good" infant or saving a severely impaired one—is necessarily to be avoided at all costs. Doctors employing this strategy err in both directions, though they seek, through clinical observations, to minimize each type of mistake. However, while there is an ethical reason to begin treatment, there is no equally com-

pelling reason not to pull back once a child's prognosis appears poor.[18]

By contrast, American neonatologists tend to treat aggressively until it is very plain that the infant will not survive or that the treatment is simply cruel. Rhoden maintains that physicians using this approach "will increasingly be governed by technology instead of employing it as a tool"[19] That, combined with the uneasiness Americans generally feel about withdrawing even useless treatment, makes American medicine easy prey for the technological imperative.

Deciding which infants should not be treated is only the first problem. Who should have ultimate decision-making authority is just as fiercely argued. A policy of treating all infants who are not dying automatically puts the decision making in the hands of neonatologists; only they have the expertise to determine if an infant is in fact dying. Where a policy of selective nontreatment, like Britain's, is adopted, some nonetheless recommend that decision making remain in the hands of neonatologists. They point out that treatment decisions about severely handicapped infants have to be made quickly. There is simply not enough time for parents to absorb their distress and begin, as most parents will, to formulate their plan for providing the special care their child will need. Physicians are in a better position to keep the principle of nonmaleficence in its medical context.

If a policy of selective nontreatment is adopted, it can also allow for decision making shared by neonatologists and parents or for decision making by parents alone. Taking the middle ground, some would limit parental decision making only to those cases, like that of the Houles' son, in which treatment may not benefit the infant beyond possibly saving his or her life. In such cases, the parents' willingness to commit themselves to the child or shoulder the burdens the child would place on the family as a whole could legitimately be considered.

Still others hold that all treatment decisions are ultimately for the parents to make. Leaving treatment decisions to parents would make the lack of uniformity in treatment decisions even more common than it already is. However, advocates of parental decision making point out that parents are the ones who will live with their decision—be it to fight for or to let go of the life of their infant—for the rest of their lives.

Barbara Katz Rothman would put parents in control of decision making as a safeguard against bureaucratization of ethical decisions:

> It is not really a question of whose judgment we trust. We cannot know who will be right, but we do know that, inevitably, anyone making these decisions will sometimes be wrong. To me it comes down not to whose *judgment* we trust but whose *mistakes*. . . .
>
> Why then do I trust the idiosyncratic mistakes of parents? Precisely because they are idiosyncratic. The mistakes of medicine and those of the state are systematic, and that alone is reason not to trust. Medicine and (perhaps even more so) the state make their mistakes in their own interests, in calculations of cost-benefit ratios, in definitions of "salvageability," in the very drawing of lines.[20]

Any treatment policy involving infants, however it is drawn up, cannot accommodate the principle of autonomy. Infants are incompetent in the same sense that the comatose, senile, or retarded are, because they cannot take part in the decision. But their incompetence is thoroughgoing, for infants have no personal history that might give a clue to what they would want, what they can accomplish in spite of their handicaps. Although handicaps do not obliterate personality, all newborns—abnormal and normal alike—are in some sense ciphers. Whether they will approach life with optimism or pessimism, whether they will struggle to best life's problems or simply resign themselves to defeat, these are aspects of temperament that remain unknown for years.

As a consequence the quality of life that a handicapped child might expect exerts a particularly strong pressure. Criticism of the decisions being made in neonatal intensive care units often centers on the perception that they have been thoroughly muddied by quality-of-life considerations. Neonatologists have their own personal views about what conditions would make life intolerable. So, too, do parents. Further, many are convinced that parents who consider quality of life consider their own, not their infant's, quality of life. They cite the Johns Hopkins Hospital case as proof of that. The question of quality of life is at play in decisions about treatment for adults. There, however, it has been pressed into service to justify one's right to die, as in the cases of Karen Quinlan and Nancy Cruzan. For infants, quality of life is pressed into service to defend both the right to die, as in the case of Andrew Stinson, and the right to life, as in the Johns Hopkins case.

Quality-of-life considerations inevitably derive from the very subjective understanding of what makes for a meaningful life. Compounding that problem, these decisions are being made by nonhandicapped people, who often forget that there is no evidence that the handicapped have a diminished instinct for life. Agreeing that there are cases when treatment is not beneficent, many believe that better decisions are made when a test is used that tries to consider what is in the patient's best interests. There is a subtle but important distinction here. The advantage of a best-interests test lies in its bringing the question back to the infant and only the infant. Accepting the fact that a handicapped infant will not have the same quality of life a nonhandicapped person could expect, one asks if that life would not still be worth living even with the handicaps. Best interests are judged within the context of the infant's condition.

If we accept the proposition that some infants are so severely handicapped that efforts to prolong their lives are not beneficent, then we must deal with the problem of how to care for them until they die. Based on his experience with infants with spina bifida, John Lorber describes what he believes is entailed when a child is allowed to die:

> It means the provision of normal tender nursing care . . . with ordinary feeding but no more; no incubators, no oxygen, no tube feeding, and no antibiotic drugs. To deny an infant the potential benefit of an operation and then prolong life by other means is irrational.[21]

What happens when an infant who is allowed to die does not die? Dying can be encouraged. For example, an infant can be so oversedated that he or she never wakes to cry for food. A corruption of the meaning of allowing an infant to die, this is in fact infanticide.

Infanticide—the word alone mobilizes strong emotions. We fancy that infanticide has no place in our society, in our time. Cases in which infanticide might be at issue are rarely prosecuted. Indeed, no state has a law that specifically deals with infanticide, although all states protect children under child abuse and neglect statutes.

Infanticide did not arise with the development of neonatology. The ancient Greeks left handicapped newborns on a mountain, to die of exposure or be eaten by animals. Before the advent of neonatology, physicians often left live-born but severely handicapped infants to die in the delivery room. But neonatology has brought the question of infanticide out into the open.

Infanticide has been justified on the grounds that newborns who are not treated or cannot be treated often suffer a painful, long-drawn-out dying. For those infants infanticide would be a form of euthanasia. Because it would be involuntary, it would profoundly affect others, either saddling them with guilt or providing longed-for, speedy release. Commenting on the slow starvation of the Down's syndrome child born at the Johns Hopkins Hospital, Joseph Fletcher asserted that "some form of direct termination would have been far more merciful as far as the infant, nurses, parents, and some of the physicians were concerned."[22]

Philosopher Michael Tooley defends infanticide on grounds that newborns do not count as persons. For Tooley personhood requires the following:

1. A capacity for desires about one's future
2. A capacity to have a concept of a self
3. The actuality of being a conscious subject of experiences
4. A capacity for self-consciousness
5. The actuality of being a continuing subject of experiences and other mental states.[23]

One of the problems with Tooley's criteria is that they can be applied to all newborns, normal and abnormal alike. If a normal infant's potential for personhood keeps us from killing that child, then the handicapped infant's potential for personhood, however diminished, should likewise keep us from killing that child.

To many the whole discussion of personhood seems simply an artful dodge designed to anesthetize our emotional response to newborns. Handicapped or not, infants are real, and they are a part of our world. They should not have to meet an impossible standard of personhood to have a claim to our care. Who should be treated? Who should not? How will we care for the infants whose best interests call for nontreatment? How we respond to that claim will depend not on our personhood but on our humanity. We owe these newest, most fragile members of the community the finest of decisions made on their behalf. And we owe ourselves a clear-eyed acknowledgment of how and why we make and carry out those decisions.

BIOETHICS AND COSTS

Ironically, just when biomedicine has given us opportunities to overleap disease and the body's degeneration, scarce resources have impeded the jump. That irony is at play in every area of our health care system, but the classic example is that of the care for kidney failure.

Hemodialysis, by which a machine takes over for the kidneys to cleanse the blood of substances the body usually excretes, was first used in the 1940s to help patients get through a crisis in kidney function. In 1960 the technology was refined so that dialysis could be done not just as a stopgap measure but on a long-term basis. Dialysis could provide a kind of time-out for those waiting for a transplant, or it could sustain a patient with kidney failure for the rest of his or her otherwise normal life.

For patients and their families, the ability to treat kidney failure can have its trying side. Emotional difficulties can come hand in hand with the treatment regimen. Those on dialysis often find despotic the strict diet, the periods of extreme fatigue, and the huge machines to which they are hooked up three times a week for six or eight hours each time. The suicide rate for dialysis patients, variously put at one hundred to four hundred times higher than the overall national rate,[1] suggests the severity of the problems.

The chance for more life when death would seem an inevitability is a miracle. As dialysis was refined, most patients considered life itself well worth the grueling treatment. The enormous expense, then as high as $20,000 a year,[2] knocked some out of the running. But many more were ready to sign up. As a consequence, no hospital could satisfy the demand for long-term dialysis. Who was to be treated? Who was to decide who was to be treated? To foster objectivity and fairness, the task of determining who would be dialyzed was often given to committees composed of physicians and members of the community. These groups, sometimes called God committees because they were making life-and-death decisions, wrestled with issues of justice in the allocation of a scarce resource.

Ideally, justice demands that all who might benefit from dialysis be offered the treatment. But that could not be. Given the scarcity of resources, a completely just use of those resources was impossible. Thus various theories of distributive justice—how to be as fair as possible to as many as possible—came into play. The inevitable consequence of scarce resources is rationing. Triage, the classification of medical cases developed in World War I by French physicians, had insinuated itself into American health care.

In triage, patients are separated into three categories: those whose wounds are so severe that they have little prospect of recovery even with medical care; those who can be saved but with extensive treatment and a long recuperation; and those whose wounds are light and who can be quickly returned to the battlefield. While triage sorts first according to medical need, the underlying assumption is one of social value: The soldier on the battlefield is more valuable than the soldier in a hospital bed. As a result, the lightly wounded were often treated first. Sometimes even the lightly wounded are bumped. For example, penicillin, a wonder drug developed during World War II but available then in very limited quantities, was given first to soldiers who had contracted venereal disease rather than to those who had light battle wounds.

Triage is an accepted practice in wartime, when national survival is at stake, but it is not easily extended as a peacetime practice. To begin, we Americans, living in a land of such staggering plenty, are incredulous that something as important as health care has to be rationed. The manner of rationing makes us just as uncomfortable. Sorting by medical need can still pass muster, but sorting by social value cannot. Lacking a single national focus as is the case in war, who is to say whether a seventeen-year-old, about to step into his or her potential, is more deserving of a scarce treatment than a forty-year-old, who has at least had a significant crack at life?

In the peacetime medical context, everyone agrees that decisions on how to allocate scarce resources must begin with likelihood of their success. Those patients who will clearly benefit from a treatment are given precedence over those who will not. After that the question becomes a free-for-all.

One camp holds that allocation decisions should be keyed to social worth. What someone has contributed to society, what that person might in future contribute—these are valid considerations in allocating scarce resources. Society has a debt to those who have or who are likely to better that society. They *deserve* those scarce resources. Allocation decisions made on the basis of social worth are also in a society's self-interest; by ensuring the survival of its most valuable members, society helps ensure its own survival.

The other camp maintains that a lottery is the only fair way to make such decisions. They grant that the lazy might not deserve the material rewards the industrious deserve, but they draw the line at life itself. Is life less precious to the derelict than it is to the executive? Comparing social worth is like comparing apples and oranges. Who has more social worth, the mother of four young children or the bachelor physicist? They worry, too, that social-worth criteria tend to take a dim view of nonconformists and dissidents. Though often pesky, nonconformists and dissidents are nonetheless essential if a society is to remain vibrant. It is they who prod society to reexamine and reshape itself.

The God committees, charged with deciding who should receive dialysis, took a variety of approaches, from allocation by social worth to allocation by queuing—first come, first served—to allocation by lottery. Committees that used social-worth criteria validated the charge that such criteria reflect traditional middle-class values: Scout leaders, churchgoers, and community volunteers were put at the top of those dialysis lists.

The God committees simply did not work. Everyone—those who made the decisions and the public at large—was intensely uncomfortable with the entire situation. In 1972, after Shep Glazer went to Washington to be dialyzed at a session of the House Ways and Means Committee, Congress voted to cover the cost of all citizens needing dialysis. Some were dismayed because they believed that Congress had not come to grips with the larger problem: national health insurance providing coverage for all major illnesses. Others believed that Congress had reacted emotionally to the dramatic demonstration of dialysis. What would happen when lobbyists for patients with cancer, multiple sclerosis, leukemia—the list is endless—came pounding on the door? Their claims are just as legitimate, but how could the government cover all of them?

Still, the legislation passed. At the time only sixty-seven hundred people were living because of a transplant or dialysis. Dr. Belding H. Scribner estimated that those who needed dialysis would stabilize at fifty thousand.[3] In fact, the program has run wildly beyond expectations. There are now some one hundred thousand people on dialysis; of those, about a quarter await or even consider the possibility of a kidney transplant.[4]

Humans, unlike cats, may not have nine lives, but many have been given more than one by virtue of the new technology known as organ transplantation. Now when a heart or liver or kidney or the like gives out, it is entirely possible to replace it.

There are four kinds of transplantation. Autografts involve tissue transplantation within the same person. Some patients who have been severely burned can now be saved when bits of skin from other parts of their bodies are set like islets in the burn area, there to take hold, extend, and seam with undamaged skin. Isografts are transplants between genetically identical individuals. They present physicians with the ideal conditions; rejection of the transplanted tissue or organ by the recipient's body is not a problem. Indeed, the first successful kidney transplant, in 1954, was between twins. Homografts are transplants within the same species. Tissue-typing and blood-typing indicate whether there is enough compatibility between patient and donor to suggest that the new organ might well be accepted. Heterografts are transplants that go across species lines. A patient with, say, a defective heart valve can be given a valve from a pig's heart.

Rejection has been a major impediment to transplantation. Most cells carry on their surface markers called antigens, lookouts that recognize foreign cells by their foreign antigens. They then order the production of antibodies. Antibodies defend the body by fighting infection, but in the case of transplantation, antibodies fight the new organ as well. Over the years, physicians have had at their disposal more and more powerful drugs to subdue patients' antigen reactions, and in the fall of 1989 it was announced that an experimental drug known as FK-506 had proved dramatically successful in early tests on liver transplants. Not only has it prevented, and even reversed, rejection, but it has done so without the side effects—damage to kidneys, raised cholesterol levels that precipitate a galloping atherosclerosis, elevated blood pressure, tremors, mood swings, hair growth in women, and swollen gums—that are common with cyclosporine, the standard antirejection drug. Dr. Thomas Starzl, head of the team that developed the drug, described FK-506 as "a miraculous drug, a wonder drug, one of those drugs that comes along once in a lifetime."[5]

If rejection can be managed or even eliminated, the number of patients who could benefit from transplantation will expand phenomenally. But with that prospect, a problem already severe in transplantation will grow worse: There are already far more people waiting for organs than there are available organs.

Every year some twenty thousand of the more than two million Americans who die have organs that could be—but are not—used for transplantation.[6] A poll conducted in 1987 found that 48 percent of the public thought that they might donate their organs.[7] Still, only about one in five Americans has completed a donor card,[8] usually on the back of a driver's license, directing that his or her organs be made available for donation. Some explain this low donation rate by noting that despite the view that it is our thinking, feeling capacities that give us our essential personhood, we retain powerful emotions about our bodies simply as bodies. The fear of mutilation is very strong, so strong that it seems almost as offensive for the dead as for the living.

Others suggest that many hesitate to sign donor cards because of an unfounded but lively fear that if they are badly hurt in an accident, their donor card might seal their doom; would a hospital trauma team, confronted with a badly hurt incompetent patient who had volunteered as an organ donor, forgo aggressive treatment?

Still others hold that signing a donor card is one of those thousands of things that take only a minute but are easily put off or forgotten. Few of us get up in the morning thinking that fate will strike us down today. A donor card can be signed tomorrow, next week, next year. With this in mind, some countries provide for presumed consent; organs may be taken for transplantation *unless* a document has been signed stating the individual's refusal to donate organs.

In the United States a number of states permit presumed consent for the donation of corneas. In all of the states donation of so-called solid organs—hearts, livers, kidneys—requires express consent, either by the donor or by the donor's family. Requiring express consent safeguards autonomy. Even in the face of a staggering shortage of organs, Americans are unwilling to override the wishes of the individual, even when the individual is dead. Medicine serves the individual, not vice versa.

The very nature of transplantation demands that great care be taken to respect the best interests of a potential donor.

"One of the fundamental precepts of ethics is that each person is an end in himself or herself, and is never to be used solely as a means to another person's ends without the agreement of the person being used," Alexander Capron observed.[9] For this reason many found unsettling the case of the Ayala family. At age fifteen Anissa Ayala was found to have leukemia. Her chance for cure was put at 70 percent if bone marrow from a compatible donor could be transplanted. Her brother was not compatible. The search for a compatible nonrelated donor, with a chance of one in twenty thousand,[10] had come to naught.

Knowing that the chances are one in four that siblings will be compatible, Abe and Mary Ayala determined to give their stricken daughter another sibling. By the time all the other odds were figured in—chances of reversing the vasectomy Abe had had; chances of Mary, over forty years old, conceiving; chances of a marrow transplant curing Anissa's leukemia—the Ayalas' plan had a 6.4 percent chance of success.[11]

Before her birth in April 1990, Marissa was known to be compatible. But to many, she appeared to have been conceived for all the wrong reasons. Although the Ayalas said that they welcomed another child, regardless of the child's compatibility as a donor, the prime purpose behind Marissa's conception was her usefulness, not the positive reasons that should spur the decision to have a child. Some went on to suggest that the Ayalas' understandable sense of desperation had compromised their ability to make medical decisions that would be in Marissa's best interests.

Others were not as emphatic. They acknowledged the ethical problems that the new technology might create. (For example, there is evidence that transplantation of fetal cells can reverse Parkinson's disease and juvenile diabetes. Will our desire to overcome these diseases lead to an acceptance of the intentional conception, then abortion of a fetus for the purpose of harvesting the fetus's potentially healing tissue?) Still, they point out that children are conceived for any number of reasons. Is the child conceived to take over the family business any less "used" than Marissa? They also sensed that the Ayalas are a solid, loving family. Perhaps Marissa, knowing that she had helped her sister in a fine, very significant way, would grow up with a powerful advantage few of us can claim.

In June 1991 Anissa received a bone marrow transplant from Marissa. A year later Anissa, so far clear of leukemia, was married. Among the guests was her doctor, Rodolf Brutoco, who remarked, "When you see Marissa walking down the aisle as flower girl, you have to realize that either girl wouldn't be here without the other."[12]

The way around situations like the Ayalas' is to build up a solid registry of potential donors. The registry is in place, but the donor lists are still thin. Americans seem to be of two minds. While we hesitate, for whatever reasons, to make arrangements for the use of our own organs, we are more disposed to consider donation of a family member's organs: 82 percent of the American public said they would do just that.[13]

Many organs were nonetheless never made available because hospital officials chose not to intrude on relatives when a family member had died. Not even asked for, the organs were often not offered. In an effort to increase the pool of available organs, federal regulations were put in place in 1987 that require all hospitals receiving Medicare or Medicaid funds—about 97 percent of the sixty-eight hundred hospitals across the country[14]—to develop procedures to identify potential organ donors and approach their families about donation. When organs become available, they are then registered in the United Network for Organ Sharing, which in turn distributes the organs on the basis of uniform criteria, including compatibility between donor and recipient, medical need, the time a patient has been waiting for an organ, and geographical proximity. Even with these regulations it is unlikely that the pool will ever be large enough to provide organs for all of the potential recipients that might benefit from a transplant.

Unquenchable entrepreneurism, such a distinctive aspect of American society, was a motivating force for one plan intended to increase the availability of organs. In 1983 H. Barry Jacobs established the International Kidney Exchange. Because the body has two kidneys but can function with only one, transplantation does not depend exclusively on someone else's death. At Jacobs's exchange, people who were willing to risk getting through the rest of their lives with only one kidney could arrange to sell the other kidney to a desperate shopper. In striking their deal, buyer and seller would arrive at a price that represented the true value of a kidney.

Jacobs's budding business, roundly criticized, never got off the ground. On the practical level, physicians expressed concern about the uncertainty of the donor's medical history, especially a problem since Jacobs intended to solicit donations from third-world citizens. That Jacobs looked to the poor for organs accounted for the strongest criticism: It is unethical to put people at risk for money. Once organ donation enters the realm of high finance, two kinds of injustice are inevitable. First, it discriminates against all but the wealthiest potential buyers. Only they have the money to be buyers of rare, therefore expensive, goods. Second, it exploits potential sellers who are poor. True, the poor are not theoretically required to make bargains that are not in their best interests. But in reality their very poverty puts them at a disadvantage in the bargaining process because they lack alternatives. Lack of alternatives drives them to the bargaining table, then strips them of the power to reject a bargain that the more advantaged might deem unwise.

One's ability to pay is nonetheless a decisive factor in transplantation. A liver transplant costs around $200,000.[15] But all medical care is expensive over the long haul. Indeed, there is a growing sense that it may be cheaper to do a liver transplant right off the bat than to provide the patient with chronic care that is ultimately more expensive because it goes on and on and on.

Scarcity of resources is a problem that goes beyond the cost of dialysis and the availability of tissue and organs for transplants. It is also a problem in terms of the dollars we as individuals and as a society can invest in health care.

In 1992 Americans spent about $838 billion for health care. That sum represented more than 14 percent of the gross domestic product[16]—the term for the dollar value of the total output of final goods and services in the nation over a year. About 60 percent is paid by private funds, either through health insurance or personal expenditure. The remainder is covered by the government—federal, state, or local—under Medicare, the program for the elderly; Medicaid, the program for the unemployed; or other health care programs for the poor.[17]

Still, a vast number of Americans have no health insurance. Eligibility requirements for Medicaid are such that some 60 percent of those with incomes below the federal poverty line are not covered.[18] Somewhere between thirty-five million and forty million Americans are medically indigent.[19] They are the working poor, ineligible for Medicaid by virtue of employment but unable to pay for health insurance by virtue of poverty. Many more who have insurance do not have enough. Faced with a major illness, they can—and often do—lose everything they own.

The extraordinary sums of money spent on health care are clearly crimping individual Americans and the nation as a whole. Fueling the alarm is the recognition that, year by year, spending on health care has been growing at a rate far and away higher than that of the economy as a whole. In 1981 American spending on health care represented 9.6 percent of the nation's economic output. Unless firmly checked, that spending is expected to increase 12 to 15 percent a year over the next five years.[20] Meanwhile, we look at other nations that spend considerably less—in 1986, when 11.1 percent of our GNP went to health care, Canada spent 8.5 percent—but have just as high health standards.[21] Further, under their systems, health care is universal—that is, available to all citizens, regardless of the individual's ability to pay. Our health care system is not only expensive, but it also has obvious, deep fissures. While many Americans receive the best medical care in the world, many other Americans receive no care at all.

Medical institutions themselves are threatened. Hospital emergency rooms have been overwhelmed. Struggling to provide more trauma care for our more violent society, many have been undone by the poor. With little money and no insurance, the poor arrive at emergency rooms when they are desperately ill because they have no family physician. In response, many hospitals have simply given up and closed their emergency rooms. Florida's Dade County has but one emergency room to serve a population of over two million.

Columbia-Presbyterian Medical Center, in New York City, is one of the country's finest teaching hospitals, but it, too, is in crisis. In the course of the 1980s it ran through more than $250 million of its $300 million endowment to cover the cost of attending to a neighborhood that is increasingly poor. Reimbursements for Medicaid patients do not meet the true costs of their care, and many other patients that the hospital cares for have no coverage of any kind. The hospital absorbs these losses. Beneficence has demanded that they be cared for; economics has demanded that the endowment fund be raided.[22]

There is no clear line between appropriate and inappropriate spending levels for health care. Is 10 percent of our GNP acceptable but 15 percent not? The more we spend on health care, the less we have for other things. For the individual, more money for health care means less money for a dinner out, a college education, travel, a home—whatever. For our society, higher spending for health care means less money for national defense, schools, libraries, roads, parks—all the things we look to government to manage, things that provide a safe environment in which we can work and flourish.

There is now a consensus that the United States has grave financial problems that threaten the standard of living and even the social cohesion of our nation. The national debt boggles the imagination; American manufacturers are having difficulty competing with foreign business; our educational system is unable to equip many students with the skills they will need to work, much less function, in an increasingly technical world; the homeless swirl slowly through our streets, while the poor live one step from desperation; across the country the infrastructure—everything from roads and bridges to sewage systems—is crumbling. These are but a few of the critical problems that beset us. Fixing them will cost money.

Deciding what percentage of the gross national product should go to health care solves only one part of the spending problem. How to divvy up what we allot for health care is another. AIDS, the frightening epidemic that first visited us in the late 1970s, has raised a host of ethical questions. Confidentiality, discrimination, limits on the obligations of health care professionals to patients, public health versus personal liberty, insurance companies' rights to assess risk, the conduct of trials on experimental drugs—all these ethical questions have been invigorated by AIDS. So, too, has the question of allocation. The Reagan administration was slow to respond to the problem—much less show even a wisp of sympathy for its victims, most of whom were homosexuals or drug users. But by 1990 the federal government's commitment to AIDS funding was $1.6 billion. Many consider that amount outsized: In 1989 forty thousand Americans died of AIDS; that same year half a million Americans succumbed to cancer, which received about the same amount of government funding. Others were just as upset, not because of the amount of money allocated to AIDS, but because two-thirds of the AIDS funding has been spent on development of drugs for those with AIDS; reiterating that AIDS can be prevented, they believe that it makes much better sense to give the lion's share of the AIDS funding to prevention rather than drug development.[23]

Concern about the costs of medical care running amok is not new, but in the early 1980s it turned to alarm and became a topic of general discussion. By then the middle class was beginning to find itself deprived of health care because of high costs. Various reasons to account for the problem were bandied about. Focusing on methods of financing, all took as their premise that the health care system was fat.

Some held that physicians' fees reflected simple avarice. Some looked to the explosion of malpractice suits and astronomical sums being awarded to plaintiffs by judges and juries. The very nature of malpractice suits had changed; it seemed that physicians were often being sued not because they had done something negligent or wrong but because things had not turned out as everyone had hoped. Whatever the reason for the suits, their number and large awards triggered appalling increases in malpractice insurance rates, which physicians passed on to patients by raising their fees. Physicians also indirectly increased the cost of health care by ordering more diagnostic testing to protect themselves from accusations of malpractice.

Efforts to control or reduce costs have been made. Competition was fostered in the hope that savvy consumers would help keep costs down. The establishment of health maintenance organizations (HMOs) was encouraged in the belief that a single institution offering a spectrum of care for a prepaid flat rate would do a better job of controlling costs. To lower hospital costs, Medicare was altered so that reimbursements were determined by the use of diagnostic-related groups (DRGs). The reimbursement for, say, an appendectomy is established. Hospitals get that reimbursement, period: If the patient is ready to go home early, the hospital keeps the change, but if the patient stays longer, the hospital must absorb the additional costs.

All of these efforts to stem the tide of health care expenditures have been to no avail. Many HMOs are in serious financial disarray. Competing to keep their enrollments up, they have been forced to add expensive services needed by only a few of their patients. While DRGs have lowered the number of days spent in the hospital, usage of nursing facilities and outpatient care after hospitalization has gone up. Critics also contend that DRGs have forced hospitals to discharge some patients long before they should.

All the while, the number of people without health insurance is on the rise. Insurance companies can keep their rates down only to the extent that they can keep their reimbursements down. As medical costs exploded, insurance companies became more and more selective, excluding from their pools older people, people at risk of illness because of their physical condition or occupation, or people with past health problems. For them, insurance was available but at very high rates, which many could not afford.

Analyzing health care costs, Daniel Callahan believes that they will never be controlled if we continue to view the problem as one simply of waste and inefficiency. He believes that we will not be able to control costs for health care until we absorb the implications of biomedicine.

At the beginning of the twentieth century the major causes of death were infectious diseases. By the middle of the century biomedicine had essentially overcome those. As a consequence, people are living longer. Indeed, the elderly now make up the fastest-growing segment of the American population. It is estimated that those sixty-five years old and up will grow from 11.7 percent of the population in 1985 to 22 percent in the year 2035.[24]

Thus chronic illness, especially heart disease and cancer, and the various dementias common to the elderly are today's major health problems. They have yielded to biomedicine only in part, and grudgingly at that. It is not for want of trying. Trillions of dollars have been put into biomedicine, and the medical community has taken up the challenge of making chronic diseases a thing of the past.

In the process, we have lost sight of reality. Biomedicine

has given us better health and longer life than our grand-parents expected. But we have come to believe that good health is the *one* essential for a meaningful life—a belief refuted by people like Stephen Hawking, who, confined to a wheelchair and unable to speak, is nonetheless an eminent theoretical physicist.

Callahan concludes that efforts to control health care costs will be to no avail if we insist that with more knowledge and still more sophisticated technology, we can gain complete control over the human body. In the thrall of medical technology, we consciously or unconsciously expect that biomedicine will one day cure death. It simply cannot be. Callahan's logic leads inexorably to a complete rethinking of our health care needs:

> If . . . we believe it is fitting in the name of other societal goods to limit our aspirations for improved health, and thus also our healthcare resources, we seem to be resigning ourselves to a course close to old-fashioned fatalism. That course means, it would seem, an acceptance of avoidable suffering and death. . . .
>
> It is [a] course we must risk. We cannot avoid it. . . . We need a healthcare system that can learn better how to meet the abiding human need for care, develop moderate and feasible aspirations for cure, and come to see the value of living within restricted frontiers.[25]

For Callahan, care is the basis for a good and just health care system. At the turn of the century, physicians laid their emphasis on care because their ability to cure was so restricted. Physicians now have many technologies by which to cure, but getting and using those technologies has relegated care to a lower station. The dire shortage of facilities and services for the chronically ill, the handicapped, the retarded, and the mentally ill suggests that care is slipping out of the health care equation.

That people ultimately need and want care surely accounts for the success of the hospice movement. Ironically, it has in some instances taken hold despite opposition from the traditional health care community. An organization that provides care for the terminally ill, hospice helps families care for the dying at home, although some hospices have an inpatient facility for patients whose care is beyond their families' ability to provide. Hospice is decidedly low tech. There is no aggressive treatment. Instead, palliation is emphasized. In fact, hospice has led the medical community as a whole in developing a use of drugs to relieve pain while maximizing the patient's lucidity. Finally, hospice views meeting the social, emotional, and spiritual needs of both patient and family as essential components of its work. Care is even extended to families after the patient has died, in the form of a bereavement program.

That care is slipping out of the health care equation is evident not just in the case of the terminally ill. Many infants are discharged from neonatal intensive care units alive but so handicapped that institutionalization is required. But where are those institutions, and who will pay for their expensive services? If sanctity of life is truly a value we mean to affirm, we must give it play beyond acute-care hospital settings. Even if we choose to temper sanctity of life with considerations of quality of life, long-term care must be strengthened.

The case of Larry McAfee serves as a good example. In 1985 McAfee became a quadriplegic as a result of a motorcycle accident. Sustained by a ventilator, he found that there was nothing that made his life worth living. Never again could he hunt or ride his motorcycle, and how could he continue to work as a mechanical engineer? The prospect of such a barren existence, endured in a nursing home, filled McAfee with despair. Medicare would pay for care in a nursing home, but it would not pay for care in any other setting. In this kind of case, the system unwittingly subverts its own goals and potential efficiencies: Helping him live more on his own would give McAfee an enlarged life, and it would come at a lower cost. These situations inevitably give rise to dark conclusions, deserved or undeserved. Paul Longmore observed that

[b]y failing over the past several years to let him exercise his right to independent living and self-determination, the State of Georgia, in effect, has been telling Larry McAfee, "People like you are better off dead." He got the message.[26]

In 1989 McAfee appealed to the Georgia Superior Court to assert his right to turn off his ventilator and die. The court agreed, with the proviso that the state's supreme court affirm the decision, which it did.

In mid-1991 McAfee was still alive, though he has said all along, "Turning off the ventilator still remains a very viable option to me."[27] His decision to put off suicide was the result of the extensive publicity generated by his court case. He was taken into a project that trains the severely handicapped in the use of voice-activated computers, which could lead to work in computerized design and drafting. Then McAfee still had to badger the system for a waiver to use Medicaid funding to live outside of an institution.

Daniel Callahan sums up the problem of quality of life

and its relationship to medical technology, and he proposes a solution:

> A powerful proclivity toward acute-care, high-technology medicine has . . . meant the neglect of those conditions that do not shorten life but significantly reduce its quality. . . . A primary question always to be asked is: If we are to have available life-saving therapies and technologies, do we have in place other follow-up therapies and forms of care that ensure a good long-term quality of life? If the answer to that question is no, then there should be a strong reluctance to disseminate that therapy until such a standard can reasonably be assured.[28]

Yet another shift in the nature of our health care system is the comparatively new emphasis on the individual. The great improvements in health up to the beginning of this century were due in large measure to improvements in sanitation, nutrition, and general living conditions—all aspects of public health and preventive medicine. Biomedicine focuses on individual patients after they have become ill. Many believe that we have missed any number of opportunities to improve everybody's health by investing so heavily in individualized, interventionist care. Consider Rick Carlson's ranking and weighting of the variables influencing health: Most important is environment, followed next by life-style, then society, genetics, and finally medical care. By his calculation, medical care accounts for only 6 percent of what makes for good health.[29] If Carlson's evaluation is even remotely reliable, we are squandering our dollars. Instead of building more neonatal intensive care units, we should be cleaning up our polluted air, soil, and waterways. Instead of trying to devise artificial hearts, we should be teaching the fundamentals of good nutrition.

The pressures built up by the crushing expense of health care may come to temper how we frame our ethical debates. In January 1990, only weeks after the death of Nancy Cruzan, ethicists were startled to learn of the case of Helga Wanglie. The eighty-seven-year-old woman had lain unconscious in Hennepin County Medical Center, sustained by a ventilator and feeding tube, for eight months. Having determined that she would never recover, physicians proposed that her ventilator be turned off. Wanglie's husband and two children refused consent. "She doesn't know anybody or anything," Oliver Wanglie acknowledged. But he went on to say that his wife had made clear not long before her illness that she would want to be aggressively treated: "She told me, 'Only He who gave life has the right to take life.' "[30]

Ethicists could think of no other case in which it was hospital administrators who went to court to ask permission to end what they considered futile treatment. "We've all worked long and hard for the patient's right to say stop," Susan Wolf commented. "That leaves the lurking question of whether it's a symmetrical issue and they also have the right to say do everything indefinitely, even when the doctors believe it's futile."[31]

Here the principle of autonomy as we have come to understand it was threatened. Helga Wanglie had explicitly voiced her desires, and her family wanted to honor them. In July 1991 a judge ruled against the hospital. Helga Wanglie, kept on the ventilator, died soon after.

Wanglie's autonomy was being challenged by her physicians' view of nonmaleficence, but it is easy to see another patient's autonomy being challenged by considerations of economics. Will hospitals, concerned about the best use of their facilities, and insurance companies, concerned about keeping their reimbursements down, start demanding withdrawal of treatment?

Ignoring the immediate needs of the individual is very, very hard. It is simple human nature that the cries of a person before us have an emotional heft that nameless, faceless, statistical people of the future do not evoke. Ignoring the immediate needs of the individual is especially hard for Americans. Believing that by fostering the good of the individual we foster the good of our society, we have developed and shaped our social structures so as to give the individual the greatest latitude.

Coby Howard was seven years old when his leukemia was diagnosed in mid-1987. Bone marrow transplants were the one form of treatment for his disease. But the operation costs $100,000 to $200,000, and earlier in the year the state of Oregon had decided to end Medicaid funding for all transplants except those of corneas and kidneys. The money saved by limiting transplantation would extend prenatal care to fifteen hundred women.

Scrambling to raise money for Coby, his family and friends had collected $70,000 when Coby died at the end of the year. His death, reported in the media across the nation, became an anguishing emblem of the inequities of our health care system. So strongly do we feel about denial of health services because of an inability to pay that it hardly matters that Coby had at the very beginning been considered unsuitable for a bone marrow transplant. Another Oregon resident who might well benefit from but cannot afford a transplant would come along all too soon.

Americans are of two minds about health care. A 1987 Harris survey found that 91 percent of the public believes that "everybody should have the right to get the best possible healthcare—as good as the treatment a millionaire gets."[32] At the same time, a survey by the Public Agenda Foundation found that a majority believes that the government should set up a program to cover catastrophic illness, but nine out of ten of those polled balked if such a program would increase each person's taxes by about $125 a year.[33] We cannot have it both ways.

In the meantime much of the fat has been cut out of the health care system, and yet the cost is high and soaring higher. Excitement about the possibilities of biomedicine has only recently been tempered by concern about its cost. There is much talk about making hard choices, but we are only beginning to do it. Oregon's decision to restrict Medicaid funds for most transplants was undoubtedly a hard choice. It still does not provide basic health care for all who need it; rather, one form of rationing has been replaced by another. Was it a good choice or even the best of unpalatable choices?

The next step in Oregon's plan to restructure health coverage serves as an example of the complexities, anxieties, and setbacks that will come with rethinking health care. To cover all of its citizens, it was proposed that employers insure permanent employees and their dependents and the state expand its Medicaid program to cover all of the poor, not just the poorest of the poor. To pay for health care for another 120,000 people,[34] the state would limit what it would cover.

After consulting with leaders in the medical profession, business, and labor and, through town meetings, with the general public, the Oregon Health Services Commission drew up a list of medical procedures ranked according to efficacy and cost. In 1991 the legislature approved the plan, including financing for the first 587 entries in the 709-item list. Liver transplants for alcoholics, aggressive treatment for newborns weighing less than 500 grams, and aggressive treatment for terminally ill AIDS patients—these are some of the treatments that did not make the cut.

Because the plan would necessitate changes in Medicaid, approval by the federal government was required. But the Bush administration balked, saying that the Oregon plan discriminated against the disabled. A number of groups—among them the Children's Defense Fund and the National Right to Life Committee—had reservations about the plan, but many saw the administration's rejection as a political move made with an eye to the 1992 elections, to be held just three months later; the Department of Health and Human Services had been considering the plan for almost a year but had never mentioned such a concern before making its ruling public. The charge of discrimination was stoutly challenged by the state. Governor Barbara Roberts took the lead:

> My husband is a paraplegic and one of my sons is autistic. I have spent my life working as an advocate for people with disabilities. As Governor, I would not have supported a plan that compromised their rights and needs.[35]

Setting priorities in health care has begun with the vulnerable poor, who account for only a part of our nation's health care costs. If health care is skewing our total spending, we need a thoroughgoing reordering of our health expectations for all members of our society. Only then will we have a health care system that is just and humane.

PERSONAL RULES, SOCIETY'S RULES

Abortion. The very word raises most Americans' hackles. For decades now we have bitterly wrangled over this issue. On one side are the pro-life forces. Their position rests on the premise that from conception on, the unborn is a human being with a right to life; abortion is nothing less than killing an innocent person. As such, it must by proscribed. Arrayed in opposition are the pro-choice forces. Their position denies that the embryo or fetus is a human being deserving legal protection, with rights that supersede those of the mother; abortion, they maintain, is a private matter, the province of the woman, not of the state.

Pro-life, pro-choice, the movements are not as simple as their stated positions would indicate. The pro-life movement attracts some who have difficulty envisioning the unborn as human beings deserving protection. Still, an event—conception—has occurred for which responsibility must be taken; the time to make decisions about having children is before they are conceived, not after. Others disapprove of all sexual intercourse that is not for procreation and especially of sex outside of marriage. They believe that abortion exacerbates both.

As for pro-choice advocates, many are not much moved by the claim that a woman has a right to make decisions concerning her own body. Rather, they join the cause because they worry about the strains on our society that come of unwanted or neglected children. Look at all the welfare mothers, many of them teenage children themselves, who with their unplanned children survive only because of public assistance. Look, too, at crack babies, the flotsam and jetsam of their addicted mothers. Others, seeing our society's suffocation by overpopulation as a real and immediate possibility, look to abortion as one way to keep population within bounds.

Complicating matters, the two movements have staked out the extremes of a continuum on which most Americans fall somewhere in the middle. Some would permit abortion only when the mother's life is at risk. Some would permit abortion only in cases of rape or incest. Some would permit abortion when prenatal defects are diagnosed but not when having a child seems simply inconvenient. Some would permit abortion to end an inconvenient pregnancy but not as a means of sex selection. These are only a few of the what-ifs and yes-buts that temper opinions. Logic might call for an all-or-nothing policy: If abortion is the taking of human life, opposition to abortion would allow for no exceptions; if abortion is not the taking of human life, support for abortion would permit no restrictions. But for Americans the abortion debate mobilizes emotional responses that refuse to kowtow to logic. Most Americans want abortion to be available but with restrictions.

*　　*　　*

The pro-life and pro-choice positions sink or swim on the status of the unborn. Is the zygote, embryo, or fetus an actual human being, or is it a potential human being? If it is a potential human being, what are its rights compared with those of an actual human being? Just when does human life begin?

Even the scientific community does not answer that with a single voice. In genetic terms, human life begins at conception. Sperm and ovum unite to form the zygote, with twenty-three chromosomes contributed by the sperm and twenty-three by the ovum. The single-celled zygote contains the complete genetic code for a being at once like every other member of the human species and still utterly unique.

Many scientists do not accept conception as the threshold of human life. They point out that all of the body's nucleated cells have the same forty-six chromosomes. A single cell of the heart is merely a cell of the heart, not a human being. Genetic completeness is meaningless without physiological, experiential, and social capacities.

After fertilization, cell division begins, transforming the zygote into a preembryo. Floating free in the mother's body, the preembryo wafts from the fallopian tube, where conception takes place, to the uterus, where the preembryo implants itself in the wall of the uterus and sparks the development of the placenta. This phase is perilous. It is estimated that half of all preembryos fail to implant and so die before new life is even recognized.[1]

Once implantation has taken place, the embryonic phase commences. Even at this point, pairs of embryos can meld, producing one normal embryo. Just as mysteriously, a single embryo can divide into several identical embryos. Legalists take this fact to claim that conception cannot be the beginning of human life if one zygote might naturally turn into several embryos or several zygotes naturally turn into one.

Embryonic activity centers primarily on the formation of organs. At the end of the eighth week from fertilization, the embryonic stage gives way to the fetal stage. The human body is laid out, and although rudimentary, it is beginning to function as a human body. The heart is pumping, brain activity can be detected, and there is movement, even though it will be several months more before quickening—the mother's first feeling of fetal movement. Some scientists set the beginning of human life here.

Others hold that human life requires psychic capacities, the operation of some sense of inner experience. Can the fetus feel pain? That is not known. However, scientists rule out the possibility for the first thirteen weeks, or trimester, of gestation. They go on to say that psychic awareness is unlikely until the twentieth—some believe the thirtieth—week.

Still others see socialization as the sine qua non of human life. They place the beginning of life at birth or even later, as defined by the ability to recognize other human beings or to use language.

Nonscientists have as wide a range of opinions as scientists. Saint Augustine held that human life begins at quickening, which occurs in the fourth or fifth month of pregnancy. Saint Thomas Aquinas, like Aristotle, set the beginning of human life at the time when the unborn is given a soul: For males, ensoulment was believed to occur forty days after conception; for females, eighty days. Saint Gregory of Nyssa, like Plato, set the beginning of human life at conception. Only in the late 1800s, when fertilization was first understood, did the Roman Catholic church give up ensoulment and settle on conception as the beginning of human life.

*   *   *

Every day thousands of women destroy the actual or potential human beings they carry within their bellies. Why?

Indications—the medical term for the symptoms that call for a given therapy—for abortion fall into several categories. Maternal health indications comprise all of those physical problems that might, if exacerbated by a pregnancy or birth, destroy the health of or kill the mother. The Roman Catholic church permits therapeutic abortion in only two cases: for an ectopic pregnancy, in which development is occurring in the fallopian tube rather than the uterus; and for uterine cancer. The church justifies abortions under these circumstances by its principle of double effect: Treatment is the removal of the fallopian tube or the uterus; the death of the conceptus is a foreseen but unintended consequence of that treatment. In any other situation, the direct form and purpose of therapeutic abortion is the removal of the unborn. As such, it is illicit. If the mother will die, so be it. The church holds that abortion on maternal life indications destroys our necessary belief in a mother's total dedication to each child. If she is willing to sacrifice one child to save herself, can her other children truly believe that she would not sacrifice them to save herself?

Many people who strongly oppose abortion are nonetheless persuaded that abortion is appropriate when the mother's health is in jeopardy. Polling in 1989 found that 88 percent of Americans support therapeutic abortions.[2] History and literature are chock full of people who have given their own lives to save others, but there is no ethical system that demands that a person die in order to save another. Forcing a woman to continue with a pregnancy that may kill her holds a woman to a standard that is both harsh and exceptional. Further, critics of the Roman Catholic reasoning see it as an extreme narrowing of the larger sphere of family that a woman lives in. Will her other children derive any comfort from their dead mother's heroic abandonment of herself and them?

Ironically, for all that the phrase "to save the life of the mother" is bandied about in today's debate, abortions on maternal health indications are rare. With the new medical technology, physicians can manage even very serious maternal health problems. Indeed, some physicians say that there is no maternal health problem that cannot be managed.

The gray area between maternal health and maternal life is well illustrated by the case of Nancy Klein, who was about ten weeks pregnant when she was in an automobile accident on 13 December 1988. Her physicians doubted that she would live, much less regain consciousness, but believed that an abortion would improve her chances. Because Klein was in a coma and could not give informed consent, hospital officials would not permit an abortion to be performed without consent from a court-appointed guardian.

In court some physicians testified that pregnancy so increases the risks for a comatose patient that it might kill Klein. Other physicians testified that while pregnancy increases risks for a comatose patient, it is not life-threatening. At the same time, John Short and John Broderick, two pro-life activists, vied with Martin Klein for guardianship of his wife and of the fetus she was carrying. After two unsuccessful appeals of the ruling giving Martin Klein guardianship, the abortion was performed.

A year later Klein was out of the coma but still in the hospital, and it was not clear if she would fully recover. The abortion allowed her physicians to use stronger medications and pursue a more aggressive rehabilitation program. But who is to say that it was the abortion that accounts for her astonishing improvement?

Spontaneous abortion, or miscarriage, often occurs because the fetus is abnormal. Medically induced abortion performed on fetal indications—evidence of fetal abnormalities that have not precipitated a miscarriage—is a fairly recent phenomenon; the means to evaluate the fetus are the product of the new medical technology. Congenital defects have various causes. Some, like cystic fibrosis, come of inherited disorders; some, like spina bifida, come of prenatal development gone awry. Still others are caused by teratogens, external agents that upset the normal development of the unborn. Rubella was the first recognized teratogen. In 1941 Norman Gregg, an ophthalmologist, made the connection between congenital blindness and the mother's exposure to German measles during the first three months of pregnancy.

In 1962 Americans took up the morality of abortion on fetal indications, using the case of Sherri Finkbine. During the second month of her pregnancy, she had taken thalidomide, a sleeping pill that her husband had gotten while in London.

At the time, thalidomide was awaiting approval by the Food and Drug Administration (FDA) and so was not generally available in the United States. Reports on its use in animal studies gave no indication that the drug might have undesirable side effects, but those reports also showed that thalidomide did not make the animals fall asleep. That gave the FDA's Frances Kelsey pause. Wondering about other differences in the drug's effect on animals and humans, Kelsey asked the manufacturer for more tests.

Soon after Finkbine used thalidomide, news of the rash of European babies with birth defects caused by the drug—ranging from missing or short, flipperlike limbs and missing or displaced organs—reached the United States. By August 1962 an estimated eight thousand European babies affected by thalidomide had been born.[3]

The law in most states at that time permitted abortion only to save the life of the mother. Her situation not meeting the law's criteria, Finkbine went to court to obtain a declaratory judgment that would protect her, her physician, and the hospital from prosecution for an illegal abortion. But her plea was dismissed, so Finkbine went to Sweden to have an abortion. The fetus was indeed abnormal.

Since then the list of identified teratogens has grown astronomically. Amniocentesis, available since the 1970s, and chorionic villi assay, available since the 1980s, have given reliable proof of the presence of many of the more than three thousand genetic defects now cataloged. Ultrasound is another technology that has given physicians a once unimaginable look at the developing unborn. As the technology is further refined, abortions on fetal indications could mushroom.

Many—70 percent of the American public[4]—regard such abortions as a merciful release for all: The fetus is saved from a life of frustration, misery, and pain; the family is saved from the often impossible task of helping the child live a comfortable life with some degree of meaning; society is saved the enormous expense of caring for the handicapped.

Some nonetheless abhor abortions performed on fetal indications. The religious view each human as God's purposive creation, with which we have no right to tamper. Others point out that amniocentesis can detect the presence but not the severity of, say, Down's syndrome. They remind us that there are all about us happy, truly accomplished people who also happen to be handicapped. Further, many attest that the great burden of caring for a handicapped family member is more than made up for by the ways it has enriched their lives. Many handicapped people themselves oppose abortion on fetal indications. They see in it a growing intolerance of any imperfection, an attitude that in turn fosters the mechanisms for actively excluding the handicapped. Many warn that as future technology offers even closer prenatal scrutiny of the unborn, abortion on fetal indications will become hypercritical or forced. Fetuses with mild or cosmetic abnormalities may be aborted. Women, even those who wish to continue the pregnancy, may be forced to abort by a society bent on protecting itself from the enormous, potentially crushing costs of caring for the handicapped.

Abortions are also performed on so-called humanitarian indications, for women who have conceived as a result of rape or incest. Even many who generally disapprove of abortion believe that to require a woman to continue a pregnancy resulting from rape or incest, in which the embryo or fetus is a kind of aggressor, too, is cruel. The strict pro-life position maintains that the unborn child is wholly innocent. "Rape and incest are tragedies, but why visit on the second victim, the unborn child that is the product of that criminal act, capital punishment?" asked Congressman Henry Hyde.[5] Others hold that women who continue pregnancies resulting from such violence draw at least something good from an otherwise horrifying encounter. Eighty-two percent of the public,[6] including many who strongly disapprove of abortion, nonetheless favor exceptions on these grounds.

Maternal health or life indications, fetal indications, humanitarian indications: These account for a minuscule portion of the staggering number—approximately 1.6 million[7]—of abortions performed each year in the U.S. Maternal health indications and fetal indications each account for 3 percent of the total; humanitarian indications account for 1 percent of the total.[8]

The vast majority of abortions are performed for indications that are sociological in nature. Unwed teenagers and adults, married women already swamped by the exigencies of life, these women seek abortions because they cannot see how to meet the physical, emotional, and financial demands that child-rearing entails. Edwina Davis, the wife of a physician and mother of three, became pregnant again in 1969 because her contraceptive failed. She paid $2,000 for an illegal abortion and recently said, "I simply could not have another child. My husband and I did not have the emotional energy."[9]

Fifteen years later Davis's daughter, Susan had a legal abortion that was covered by medical insurance. "I was nineteen, with one year of college," she explained. "I had dreams and plans, and wanted children when I was old enough and smart enough. I didn't feel remotely able financially to take care of a child."[10]

Pro-life supporters hold that once a human being has been conceived, that life must be respected above all else. And, they point out, there are alternatives. Charities and social service departments can assist those who wish to keep their babies. Adoption is an alternative for those who do not. Pro-choice advocates chide the pro-life forces for suggesting that our society is truly willing to accommodate these children and their families. What charities and social services there are to help these people do not begin to meet the need. In their view society shows a *disrespect* for life by demanding that these women continue their pregnancies, then providing not even a modicum of assistance essential for the proper care of the children they bear.

Exercising the right to choose does not mean that a woman will make a good choice. Pamela Carr had reservations before having an abortion at age seventeen. Those reservations ultimately crystallized into deep regret and propelled her into the pro-life movement. She remarked, "I still feel the loss of that baby, who would now be eight years old."[11]

*   *   *

Abortion is an age-old practice. Recipes for abortifacients—substances that set an abortion in motion—date back over four thousand years. The Oath of Hippocrates prohibited a physician from inducing an abortion; still, induced abortions were commonplace in Greek society of the fourth century B.C. Until the nineteenth century, what restrictions there were on abortion pertained only to the period after quickening. But beginning in the 1850s a crusade to outlaw abortion swept across the United States, and by 1880 every state had strict laws regulating the procedure. Physicians spearheaded the effort. They saw legislation first as a way to protect women from the damage or death caused by untrained abortionists. Indeed, more than half the women who had abortions in the nineteenth century died.[12] There was an ethical component of the physicans' view, as well, which came as nineteenth-century science learned more about conception and gestation. The implications of fertilization and the dizzyingly complex and rapid process of growth of a distinct human being were inescapable. Still another factor in the passage of strict abortion laws was eugenics. Some Protestants worried that the prosperous, well-educated middle and upper classes were not reproducing as much as the poor. They looked to abortion restrictions as a way to keep their numbers up.

Strict abortion laws did not put an end to abortion. So strong is the impulse to terminate an unwanted pregnancy that many women have risked criminal charges, even death, to have an abortion. Because the procedure was illegal, there are no statistics for or even good estimates of how many abortions were performed. A committee Planned Parenthood appointed in 1955 guessed that the frequency of induced abortions ranged from two hundred thousand to 1.2 million per year.[13]

In the 1960s, more than a hundred years after the big push for strict abortion laws, physicians began urging that the laws be loosened. Advances in medicine made it harder and harder for physicians to justify abortions as medically necessary. In desperation, women had turned to back-street abortionists or—especially dangerous—self-induced abortion. The role of rubella and thalidomide in birth defects made prenatal health a concern. Further, health had come to mean more than just good physical functioning. Marital difficulties, financial reversals, the demands of other children—all could affect health as much as high blood pressure. Physicians were joined by members of the helping professions—clergy, social workers, and the like—who tried to ameliorate the disastrous consequences of unwanted pregnancies, both those carried to term and those ended illegally. A refreshened feminist movement brought support from outside professional circles.

The problem with stiff abortion laws is that a large number of Americans do not buy the reasoning behind them. Some simply do not regard the unborn as fully human life. They point out that when a pregnancy ends in a spontaneous abortion—the case with perhaps one of every two zygotes that succeed to implantation[14]—no element of our society treats the abortus as a person. There are no funerals and burials; no birth or death is recorded. Tax credits can be taken only at birth. Others acknowledge that the unborn have a reality and even a significance but certainly not rights that are more significant than those of the mother. The phenomenal number of illegal abortions and a waning sense that abortion is wrong undermined the law. Ralph Potter points out,

If legal restraints against abortion are to function, they must be buttressed by inner conviction. But the conviction has decayed that abortion is an offense against God, nature, the state, one's higher self, the common weal, and the right to life.[15]

Nor do these Americans accept the notion that abortion represents the thin edge of the wedge that will inevitably lead to the disrespect of others, especially the handicapped, the infirm, and the old. Societies that have liberal abortion laws— for example, the Scandinavian countries—have not evidenced callous treatment of their vulnerable citizens.

The unraveling of restrictive abortion laws in the United States began in Texas in 1969. There Norma McCorvey sought an abortion, saying that she had been raped one evening when she was walking home from work. Texas law prohibited abortion on those grounds, but New York and California did not. Still, a legal abortion was beyond her reach, for she did not have the financial wherewithal to go to California and pay for the procedure. She then found a doctor in Texas who would provide her with an illegal abortion, but the fee, $650, was still more than she could scrape together.

A daughter was born to McCorvey in June 1970, but that would not be the end of the matter. A lawyer McCorvey talked with about adoption had introduced her to Sarah Weddington, a recent law school graduate who wanted to challenge Texas abortion law. From the start Weddington envisioned a challenge that might eventually wind up in the U.S. Supreme Court. And it did.

The case, which used the pseudonym Jane Roe to protect McCorvey and her child from publicity, was a class action suit, filed on behalf of all women—past, present, and future— seeking an abortion in Texas. It named as defendant Dallas district attorney Henry Wade, who was responsible for enforcement of the abortion laws, and charged that Jane Roe's right to make a decision about childbearing and the right to privacy in the doctor-patient relationship had been improperly thwarted by Texas law. *Roe* v. *Wade* was heard by the U.S. Supreme Court in December 1971. The volatility of the issue was such that the case was reargued in October 1972.

Weddington argued that pregnancy has such a profound effect on a woman—not least because of policies of educational institutions and employers pertaining to pregnant students or workers—that it is the woman herself who should make the decision about its continuation or termination. To Weddington's assertion that the Constitution extends protection to the individual only upon birth, Texas assistant attorney general Robert C. Flowers, defending the Texas abortion law, held that life begins at conception: "If we declare, as the appellees in this case have asked the Court to declare, that an embryo or a fetus is a mass of protoplasm similar to a tumor, then of course the State has no compelling interest whatsoever."[16]

The Court's decision, handed down on 22 January 1973, was electrifying. The majority opinion, written by Justice Harry Blackmun, held that the Constitution does not cover the unborn, and though it does not specifically refer to privacy, it does imply a right of privacy through the Fourteenth Amendment's protection of personal liberty. The decision held that a state has no right to meddle in a woman's decision to have an abortion in the first trimester of the pregnancy; it is a private matter to be decided by the woman in consultation with her physician. During the second trimester, a state might regulate abortion but only insofar as laws and regulations were designed to protect maternal health. From the point of viability on, when the fetus might survive outside the mother's body, a state's right to protect third parties—in this case the fetus—from injury allowed the state to regulate abortion closely. Still, even during the third trimester, abortion must be available to women whose life or health—physical or emotional—is threatened.

Depending on one's point of view, the decision in *Roe* v. *Wade* was either brilliant or abysmal. J. Claude Evans saw it as "a beautifully accurate balancing of individual rights gradually giving way to community rights as pregnancy continues."[17] John Cardinal Krol saw in it "disastrous implications for our stability as a civilized society."[18]

The decision in *Roe* v. *Wade*, sweeping away the stringent restrictions that most states had placed on abortion, was a devastation for the pro-life position. It did not give women an absolute right to end a pregnancy. Still, opponents of abortion could see few instances in which fetal life might be protected, and they were right. So they set about finding ways to reverse the tide. One tack, amending the Constitution, was abandoned early on. Mustering the supermajorities needed for an amendment is difficult under the best of circumstances. With Americans so divided on the issue, supermajorities were beyond reach.

Turning to political action, pro-life forces organized with remarkable determination. They made abortion the single issue for choosing one or another political candidate, and the vast amounts of money they were able to raise and invest in one or another campaign made politicians very careful indeed about their stand on abortion.

Placards with photographs of aborted fetuses were printed up for demonstrations. Gantlets of pro-lifers gathered outside abortion clinics to heckle the staff members coming to work. So-called sidewalk counselors implored women arriving for abortions to reconsider. They jammed doorways, even invaded the clinics. They used passive resistance so that police called to clear out the demonstrators could not do their job easily or quickly. Around the country, there was a rash of bombings of clinics.

The pro-choice forces had not dissolved. They, too, had demonstrations, replete with placards showing photographs of the bloody corpses of women who had died as a result of an illegal abortion. Some groups tried to foil harassment of abortion clinics. But on the political front the pro-choice forces were lackadaisical, complacent in the belief that *Roe* v. *Wade* was immune to any significant changes. Stare decisis, the principle of adhering to decided cases, is very strong in the American legal tradition. U.S. Supreme Court rulings that are overturned are rarities.

All the while, the pro-life movement was chipping away at *Roe* v. *Wade* through state and federal legislation. To be sure, the Court struck down laws requiring physicians to provide elaborate information about fetal development, about services available to mothers should they continue the pregnancy, and about child-support regulations; laws requiring a twenty-four-hour waiting period before an abortion could be performed; and laws requiring consent of the father for an abortion. But the Court let stand laws, known as the Hyde Amendments, prohibiting the use of Medicaid funds for abortions for the poor. Pro-life advocates maintain that any right to an abortion is a negative right; the individual may have the right to obtain an abortion, but society has no obligation to pay for it. Pro-choice advocates counter that the right to an abortion is meaningless if a woman cannot afford the procedure. The Court also let stand laws that prohibited abortion services in public hospitals. And in *Rust* v. *Sullivan,* handed down in 1991, it let stand regulations that prohibited any mention of abortion in counseling programs that received federal funding.

Parental consent is another battleground. Are teenagers

able to exercise informed consent properly? Pro-life advocates hold that parents should not be denied the opportunity to be responsible parents. If parental consent is necessary for a child's appendectomy, then it plainly follows that parental consent is necessary for a child's abortion. That is a position with which 70 percent of the public agrees.[19] Even more— 83 percent of the public[20]—believe that at least one parent should be at least informed before a minor has an abortion. Pro-choice advocates charge that many teenagers, frightened of wrathful or abusive parents, would thereby be forced into childbearing, something for which they are unprepared, and something that would totally disrupt their lives. The Supreme Court has let stand parental consent and notification laws so long as there is a mechanism for judicial bypass. This allows a minor to get an abortion without her parents' knowledge if she can demonstrate to a judge that she is competent to make the decision herself.

Pro-choice forces were galvanized only in 1989 when the U.S. Supreme Court heard arguments in *Webster* v. *Reproductive Health Services, Inc.* The case grew out of a 1986 Missouri law designed to discourage abortions. That law required extensive testing for fetal viability after the twentieth week, testing that many physicians consider dangerous for the pregnant woman. Another controversial provision was a ban on abortions in any public facility. Kansas City's Truman Medical Center, where nearly all Missouri abortions from sixteen weeks of pregnancy on were performed, is a private hospital, but because it is on land leased from the state, abortions would be prohibited there. What really concerned the pro-choice forces was the solicitor general's recommendation that the Court use this case as a means to reconsider and overturn *Roe* v. *Wade*. Suddenly that seemed entirely possible. Justices appointed to the Supreme Court after Ronald Reagan became president in 1981 were considerably more conservative than those who had decided *Roe* v. *Wade*. In the decision the court handed down in *Webster* v. *Reproductive Health Services, Inc., Roe* v. *Wade* was not overturned. However, the decision was otherwise a complete defeat for the pro-choice forces; laws regulating abortion no longer needed to meet a standard known as strict scrutiny. Chagrined, pro-choice advocates took a leaf from the pro-life book and began turning to legislators and legislation.

Three years later, in 1992, the Supreme Court again weighed in on abortion, this time in *Planned Parenthood* v. *Casey*. Five provisions of a Pennsylvania law regulating abortion were at issue: that a woman seeking an abortion be given information designed to encourage her to continue the pregnancy; that she then wait at least twenty-four hours before proceeding with an abortion; that teenagers obtain the consent of a parent or of a judge before having an abortion; that except in certain situations a married woman inform her husband of her intention to have an abortion; exceptions and reporting requirements for hospitals and clinics providing abortions. As in previous cases, the solicitor general asked the Court to overturn *Roe* v. *Wade*

Kathryn Kolbert, the lawyer challenging the regulations, chose a risky strategy. Believing that states could write laws that so hedged the right to abortion as to make it virtually unavailable, she asked the Court to reaffirm that the constitutional right to abortion is fundamental, thereby requiring laws regulating abortion to pass strict scrutiny. Knowing there were too few justices who viewed the right to abortion as fundamental, shunning a middle ground, Kolbert seemed a kind of latterday kamikaze. She would risk a complete defeat in the Supreme Court because that might set in motion an ultimately successful political battle.

Surprisingly, a bare majority of the Court came together to affirm the right to abortion, although it held that that right is not fundamental. Laws regulating abortion are legal as long as they do not place a so-called undue burden on a woman seeking an abortion. By that standard, the only Pennsylvania regulation found invalid was the one requiring a woman to inform her husband before having an abortion. The majority opinion analyzed anew the right to abortion—some believe that it grounded the right to abortion more securely than did *Roe* v. *Wade*—then went on to warn that the intense political pressure to overturn solid precedent imperiled the Court. One did not have to read between the lines to discern powerful tensions and unexpected realignments within the Court.

Is abortion a moral issue that should be left to the individual and her conscience, or is it a social problem that must be addressed by public policy? Pro-life advocates stoutly maintain that in *Roe* v. *Wade* the Supreme Court usurped the power of the people, through their legislators, to determine what our society will permit. From this perspective laws prohibiting abortions are essential because the practice tears the fabric of our society and coarsens us. How can we so casually end life? All this talk of "privacy" and "a woman's right to control her own body" is delusive. The unborn is not simply part of the woman's body. With its own individual genetic makeup and circulatory, nervous, and hormonal systems, it is a body residing in a body. Privacy and self-determination do not obtain when the lives of others—here, the unborn—are involved.

Pro-choice advocates contend that *Roe* v. *Wade* was an entirely proper expression of judicial power. They emphasize that each and every American has rights that the state cannot abridge, and it is the job of the judicial branch to protect those rights—it is *supposed* to be antidemocratic. True, the Constitution does not make explicit reference to abortion, or even to privacy, but the Constitution demands interpretation. Indeed, that is the reason the Constitution has retained its vitality. Defenders of the decision go on to caution that the abortion issue is a perfect example of the need to distinguish between morality and law. Good law is utterly moral, but good morality is not necessarily law. The province of law is only those areas where the peace and safety of the entire society is threatened. Glanville Williams makes the point baldly:

> There are forms of murder, or near-murder, the prohibition of which is rather the expression of a philosophical attitude than the outcome of social necessity. These are infanticide, abortion, and suicide. The prohibition of killing imposed by these three crimes does not rest upon considerations of public security.[21]

Pro-choice advocates point out that laws that do not reflect the views of society as a whole, laws that are flouted over and over again, are destructive. They, too, tear the fabric of society, as disrespect for one law blooms into disrespect for all laws.

Other pro-choice advocates warn that our constitutional separation of church and state is being breached. Evangelicals, who make up an estimated two-thirds of the pro-life movement,[22] base their position on the Bible. The Roman Catholic church's high-profile role in the abortion battle has convinced many that the church will go to great lengths to foist its doctrine on all Americans, even as many Catholics disagree with official church teaching. (The abortion rate for Catholic women is about the same as that for the population as a whole.[23]) That perception took on new life in November 1989 when Leo Maher, the Roman Catholic bishop of San Diego, denied communion to Lucy Killea, a state assemblywoman who is personally opposed to abortion but is unwilling to impose her views on others.

In fact, all religious groups are in the business of fostering and guiding their adherents' moral development. Public policies cannot help but reflect the morality of the politicians who set those policies. The Roman Catholic church was praised for excommunicating a segregationist in 1962; why, then, was it criticized in 1990 for warning Governor Mario Cuomo that because of his views on abortion, similar to Killea's, he was bound for hell? If we welcome the church's input on one matter, consistency demands that we welcome it on all matters.

There seems to be no way to reconcile all of the conflicting rights jostling for affirmation in today's abortion debate. The claim for the unborn's right to life, the claim for a woman's right to control her own body—accepting one means denying the other. One ethicist has suggested that medical technology might someday provide the valve to release the extraordinary pressure generated by the abortion debate; when it is possible to remove a five- or six-week-old embryo from the uterus and transfer it to the uterus of another woman or to an artificial womb, it would be possible to save the unborn and still satisfy a woman's decision to end a pregnancy.[24] But those are at best possibilities for the future. If transferring an embryo were possible but carried higher risks than an abortion, it would be difficult to persuade or compel women to take that course. Transfer would also open up a barely explored area of the emotional terrain of abortion: the sense that the unborn is of such little value that it can be destroyed, yet of such great value that it cannot be given to another.

There also seems to be no way to reconcile the divisive pro-life/pro-choice struggle. As though the rancor of the abortion debate is not enough, it has left us little strength with which to address other serious social problems, like education, drug abuse, the homeless, adequate health care for all. Combatants in the abortion debate shout from the extremes: no abortion under any circumstances; abortion on demand for any reason, or even no reason. Such polarization makes finding a common ground unlikely.

One thing is clear: If significant restrictions are placed on abortion, abortion will simply go underground. Strict abortion laws will surely lead to a flourishing cadre of unlicensed abortionists. The Scandinavian countries found that illegal abortions continued even when their laws were relaxed somewhat; women refused to accept the idea that their decision had to be explained to and approved by some outside authority. If RU-486, an abortifacient developed and now in use in France, becomes available in the United States, an abortion would become a considerably less dramatic medical event. Obviating the need for a surgical procedure, RU-486 sets an abortion in motion with the swallowing of a couple of pills. That prospect chills pro-life activists. Abortion as it is now performed seems all too easy; RU-486 will make it even easier for women to avoid thinking about the profound decision they have made.

The collection of cells that make up the embryo or fetus represents, even in its futurity, our history as individuals, families, a society, a species. Those cells are clearly of an order different from "a mass of protoplasm similar to a tumor." Whatever the reason for contemplating an abortion—a desperately ill pregnant woman, a violated woman, a severely handicapped fetus, a woman emotionally or socially unwilling or unable to bear or rear a child—all bespeak aspects of the human condition that we sometimes cannot, sometimes will not, ameliorate.

If abortion offends our sensibilities, if it mars our sense of what our society should be, then we cannot simply restrict or ban abortion. We must make some fundamental changes in our society. Addressing the pathology of rape and incest and strengthening the legal system that now enables rapists and molesters to brutalize with impunity; providing the medical, social, and institutional facilities needed by the handicapped; developing effective, safe contraceptives and providing education for their use; teaching children—and adults—that sexuality carries enormous responsibilities, to oneself, to one's partner, to one's offspring; alleviating the critical shortage of good day care; providing the social services for women and families in disarray so that they can welcome and care for their children—all would go far to reduce the appalling number—*1.6 million*—of abortions that are performed each year in the United States. History has shown that abortion laws alone will one way or another be gotten around, but at a price: Society is despised for its restrictions.

NOTES

Epigraph

1. Daniel Maguire, "Deciding for Yourself: The Objections," in *Ethical Issues in Death and Dying,* ed. Robert F. Weir (New York: Columbia University Press, 1977), 324.

The Principles

1. Henry David Aiken's description of the four-tiered process is to be found in "Levels of Moral Discourse," in *Reason and Conduct: New Bearings in Moral Philosophy* (New York: Alfred A. Knopf, 1962), 65–87.

2. This case is described and critiqued in Paul Ramsey, *Ethics at the Edges of Life: Medical and Legal Intersections* (New Haven: Yale University Press, 1978), 300–317, 335.

3. Quoted in "A Mother's Gift of Life," *Time,* 11 Dec. 1989, 96.

4. Tom L. Beauchamp and James F. Childress, *Principles of Biomedical Ethics,* 3d ed. (New York: Oxford University Press, 1989), 429–430.

5. Sally Johnson, "Vermont Case May Upset Transplant Policy," *New York Times,* 15 Jan. 1989.

6. Ernlé W. D. Young, *Alpha and Omega: Ethics at the Frontiers of Life and Death* (Reading, Mass.: Addison-Wesley, 1989), 30–31.

7. Beauchamp and Childress, 414.

8. Beauchamp and Childress, 84–85.

9. Quoted in Daniel Callahan, *What Kind of Life? The Limits of Medical Progress* (New York: Simon and Schuster, 1990), 34.

10. "Calm, Cool and Disconnected," *Time,* 14 May 1990, 35.

11. Joseph Fletcher, "Ethics and Euthanasia," in *Ethical Issues in Death and Dying,* 349.

Understanding Ourselves

1. Natalie Angier, "Nature May Fashion All Cells' Proteins from a Few Primordial Parts," *New York Times,* 11 Dec. 1990.

2. Kerryn Brandt, research associate, Genome Data Base, telephone conversation with author, 19 January 1993.

3. Clifford Grobstein, *Science and the Unborn: Choosing Human Futures* (New York: Basic Books, 1988), 137–138.

4. Stacey FitzSimmons, assistant medical-scientific director, Cystic Fibrosis Foundation, telephone conversation with author, 15 January 1993.

5. Quoted in Leon Jaroff, "The Gene Hunt," *Time,* 20 Mar. 1989, 67.

6. Jaroff, 63.

7. FitzSimmons.

8. Gena Corea, *The Mother Machine: Reproductive Technologies from Artificial Insemination to Artificial Wombs* (New York: Harper and Row, 1985), 188.

9. Dorothy C. Wertz and John C. Fletcher, "Fatal Knowledge? Prenatal Diagnosis and Sex Selection," *Hastings Center Report* 19 (May/June 1989): 21.

10. Elizabeth Greenhall and Martin Vessey, "The Prevalence of Subfertility: A Review of the Current Confusion and a Report of Two New Studies," *Fertility and Sterility* 54 (December 1990): 983.

11. The Vatican doctrinal statement "Instruction on Respect for Human Life in Its Origin and on the Dignity of Procreation: Replies to Certain Questions of the Day," *New York Times,* 11 March 1987.

12. Philip Elmer-DeWitt, "Making Babies," *Time,* 30 Sept. 1991, 58.

13. Quoted in Ronald Smothers, "Embryos in a Divorce Case: Joint Property or Offspring," *New York Times,* 22 Apr. 1989.

14. David H. Smith, *Health and Medicine in the Anglican Tradition: Conscience, Community, and Compromise* (New York: Crossroad, 1986), 78.

15. Quoted in Lori Andrews, *Between Strangers: Surrogate Mothers, Expectant Fathers, and Brave New Babies* (New York: Harper and Row, 1989), 93.

16. Quoted in Andrew H. Malcolm, "Steps to Control Surrogate Births Rekindle Debate," *New York Times,* 26 June 1988.

17. Quoted in Malcolm, "Steps."

18. Barbara Katz Rothman, *Recreating Motherhood: Ideology and Technology in a Patriarchal Society* (New York: W. W. Norton, 1989), 238.

19. Paul Ramsey, *Fabricated Man: The Ethics of Genetic Control* (New Haven: Yale University Press, 1970), 33–34.

20. Joseph Fletcher, *Morals and Medicine* (Princeton: Princeton University Press, 1954), 121.

Bioethics at the End of Life

1. Quoted in Andrew H. Malcolm, *This Far and No More: A True Story* (New York: Times Books, 1987), 79.

2. Leonard L. Bailey, "Organ Transplantation: A Paradigm of Medical Progress," *Hastings Center Report* 20 (January/February 1990): 26.

3. Robert S. Morison, "Death: Process or Event?" in *Ethical Issues in Death and Dying*, 62.

4. Quoted in Nancy Gibbs, "Love and Let Die," *Time*, 19 Mar. 1990, 65.

5. Quoted in Ramsey, *Ethics at the Edges of Life*, 156.

6. Ramsey, *Ethics at the Edges of Life*, 177.

7. Jessica H. Muller and Barbara A. Koenig, "On the Boundary of Life and Death: The Definition of Dying by Medical Residents," in *Biomedicine Examined*, ed. Margaret Lock and Deborah Gordon (Dordrecht, Netherlands: Kluwer Academic Publishers, 1988), 366–367.

8. Muller and Koenig, 369.

9. George P. Fletcher, "Prolonging Life," in *Ethical Issues in Death and Dying*, 237.

10. Andrew H. Malcolm, "Weary Pioneers on the Frontier of Medical Ethics," *New York Times*, 25 Jan. 1991.

11. Malcolm, "Weary Pioneers."

12. Andrew H. Malcolm, "Right-to-Die Case Nearing a Finale," *New York Times*, 7 Dec. 1990.

13. Quoted in Beauchamp and Childress, 165.

14. Quoted in Ramsey, *Ethics at the Edges of Life*, 270.

15. Susan M. Wolf, "Nancy Beth Cruzan: In No Voice at All," *Hastings Center Report* 20 (January/February 1990): 38.

16. Wolf, 39.

17. James Bopp, Jr., "Choosing Death for Nancy Cruzan," *Hastings Center Report* 20 (January/February 1990): 42.

18. Bopp, 43.

19. Wolf, 40.

20. Gibbs, 62.

21. Quoted in Malcolm, "Right-to-Die Case Nearing a Finale."

22. Derek Humphry and Ann Wickett, *The Right to Die: Understanding Euthanasia* (New York: Harper and Row, 1986), 20.

23. Andrew H. Malcolm, "The Ultimate Decision," *New York Times Magazine,* 3 Dec. 1989, 54.

24. Humphry and Wickett, 135.

25. Quoted in Maguire, 332.

26. James F. Childress, *Priorities in Biomedical Ethics* (Philadelphia: Westminster Press, 1981), 38–39.

27. Maguire, 339.

28. Elizabeth Latimer, interview with author, 2 March 1990.

29. Beauchamp and Childress, 222.

30. Smith, 64.

31. Thomas S. Szasz, "The Ethics of Suicide," in *Ethical Issues in Death and Dying,* 374.

32. Quoted in Isabel Wilkerson, "Prosecutors Seek to Ban Doctor's Suicide Device," *New York Times,* 5 Jan. 1991.

33. Timothy E. Quill, "Death and Dignity—A Case of Individualized Decision Making," *New England Journal of Medicine* 324 (7 March 1991): 691–694.

Bioethics at the Beginning of Life

1. Robert F. Weir, *Selective Nontreatment of Handicapped Newborns: Moral Dilemmas in Neonatal Medicine* (New York: Oxford University Press, 1984), 200.

2. Ramsey, *Ethics at the Edges of Life,* 254.

3. Robert Stinson and Peggy Stinson, *The Long Dying of Baby Andrew* (Boston: Little, Brown, 1983), 92.

4. Stinson and Stinson, 341.

5. Elisabeth Rosenthal, "As More Tiny Infants Live, Choices and Burden Grow," *New York Times,* 29 Sept. 1991.

6. Weir, *Selective Nontreatment,* 69.

7. Weir, *Selective Nontreatment,* 77.

8. Weir, *Selective Nontreatment,* 240.

9. Tamar Lewin, "As the Retarded Live Longer, Anxiety Grips Aging Parents," *New York Times,* 28 Oct. 1990.

10. James J. Gustafson's "Mongolism, Parental Desires, and the Right to Life" is an eloquent, now-famous essay analyzing the decision and its implications. It is reprinted in *Ethical Issues in Death and Dying* 145–172.

11. Weir, *Selective Nontreatment,* 128–129.

12. Lawrence J. Nelson, "Perinatology/Neonatology and the Law: Looking Beyond Baby Doe," in *The Year Book of Perinatal/Neonatal Medicine,* ed. Marshall H. Klaus, M.D., and Avroy A. Fanaroff (Chicago: Year Book Medical Publishers, 1988), 6.

13. Nelson, 9.

14. Richard A. McCormick, *How Brave a New World? Dilemmas in Bioethics* (Garden City, N.Y.: Doubleday, 1981), 339.

15. Weir, *Selective Nontreatment*, 95–97.

16. Rosenthal, 26.

17. Nancy K. Rhoden, "Treating Baby Doe: The Ethics of Uncertainty," *Hastings Center Report* 16 (August 1986): 39.

18. Rhoden, 40.

19. Rhoden, 39.

20. Rothman, 193.

21. Quoted in Weir, *Selective Nontreatment*, 69.

22. Quoted in Weir, *Selective Nontreatment*, 169.

23. Weir, *Selective Nontreatment*, 153.

Bioethics and Costs

1. A suicide rate one hundred times higher than that for the general public is quoted by Jane J. Stein, *Making Medical Choices: Who Is Responsible* (Boston: Houghton Mifflin, 1978), 153. A rate four hundred times higher is quoted by B. D. Colen, *Hard Choices: Mixed Blessings of Modern Medical Technology* (New York: G. P. Putnam's Sons, 1986), 25.

2. Richard D. Lyons, "Nixon Is Reported Considering a Veto of Huge Medical and Pension Benefits Bill," *New York Times*, 22 Oct. 1972.

3. "Artificial Kidney Use Poses Awesome Questions," *New York Times*, 24 Oct. 1971.

4. Beauchamp and Childress, 206–207.

5. Quoted in Lawrence K. Altman, "Great Success with Drug in Transplants of Organs," *New York Times*, 18 Oct. 1989.

6. Beauchamp and Childress, 206.

7. Dirk Johnson, "Diverging Views Found on Donating Organs," *New York Times*, 3 May 1987.

8. Dirk Johnson.

9. Quoted in "Two Having a Baby to Save Daughter," *New York Times*, 17 Feb. 1990.

10. "JoAnne, Allison and a Cruel Promise," *New York Times*, 14 Jan. 1990.

11. "Creating a Child to Save Another," *Time*, 5 Mar. 1990, 56.

12. Quoted in "A Life-Saving Sibling Helps Out Once More," *New York Times*, 7 June 1992.

13. Dirk Johnson.

14. Robert Pear, "New Law May Spur Organ Donations," *New York Times*, 6 Sept. 1987.

15. Altman.

16. Robert Pear, "Health-Care Costs Up Sharply Again, Posing New Threat," *New York Times,* 5 Jan. 1993.

17. Callahan, *What Kind of Life?,* 268.

18. Callahan, *What Kind of Life?,* 73.

19. Callahan, *What Kind of Life?,* 73.

20. Pear.

21. Callahan, *What Kind of Life?,* 19.

22. Howard W. French, "Presbyterian Faces a Crisis of Finances," *New York Times,* 18 Dec. 1989.

23. Dick Thompson, "The AIDS Political Machine," *Time,* 22 Jan. 1990, 24.

24. Callahan, *What Kind of Life?,* 274.

25. Callahan, *What Kind of Life?,* 241.

26. Quoted in Peter Applebome, "An Angry Man Fights to Die, Then Tests Life," *New York Times,* 7 Feb. 1990.

27. Quoted in Applebome.

28. Callahan, *What Kind of Life?,* 166.

29. Childress, 75–76.

30. Quoted in Lisa Belkin, "As Family Protests, Hospital Seeks an End to Woman's Life Support," *New York Times,* 10 Jan. 1991.

31. Quoted in Belkin.

32. Callahan, *What Kind of Life?,* 84.

33. Callahan, *What Kind of Life?,* 85.

34. Philip Elmer-DeWitt, "Oregon's Bitter Pill," *Time,* 17 Aug. 1992, 45.

35. Barbara Roberts, "Bush Blows It on Health Care, *New York Times,* 11 Aug. 1992.

Personal Rules, Society's Rules

1. Grobstein, 9.

2. R. W. Apple, Jr., "Limits on Abortion Seem Less Likely," *New York Times,* 29 Sept. 1989.

3. "The Thalidomide Disaster," *Time,* 10 Aug. 1962, 32.

4. Apple.

5. Quoted in Margaret Carlson, "Abortion's Hardest Cases," *Time,* 2 July 1990, 23.

6. Apple.

7. Stanley K. Henshaw, "The Accessibility of Abortion Services in the United States," *Family Planning Perspectives* 23 (November/December 1991): 252.

8. Aida Torres and Jacqueline Darroch Forrest, "Why Do Women Have Abortions?" *Family Planning Perspectives* 20 (July/August 1988): 170.

9. Quoted in Richard Lacayo, "Whose Life Is It?" *Time*, 1 May 1989, 22.

10. Quoted in Lacayo, 22.

11. Quoted in Lacayo, 23.

12. Fred W. Friendly and Martha J. H. Elliott, *The Constitution: That Delicate Balance* (New York: Random House, 1984), 205.

13. Daniel Callahan, *Abortion: Law, Choice and Morality* (New York: Macmillan, 1970), 133.

14. Grobstein, 9, 77.

15. Ralph B. Potter, Jr., "The Abortion Debate," in *Updating Life and Death: Essays in Ethics and Medicine*, ed. Donald R. Cutler (Boston: Beacon Press, 1969), 129.

16. Quoted in Friendly and Elliott, 206.

17. Quoted in McCormick, 117.

18. Quoted in McCormick, 118.

19. Apple.

20. Apple.

21. Glanville Williams, *The Sanctity of Life and the Criminal Law* (New York: Alfred A. Knopf, 1974), x.

22. "Save the Babies," *Time*, 1 May 1989, 28.

23. "Abortion in the United States," Facts in Brief, Alan Guttmacher Institute, April 1992.

24. Young, 76.

GLOSSARY

ABORTIFACIENT. An agent that sets an abortion in motion.

ABORTION. The ending of a pregnancy.

ADENINE. One of the four nitrogenous bases that make up DNA.

AMNIOCENTESIS. A procedure for obtaining amniotic fluid for prenatal testing.

ANTIGEN. A substance on the surface of cells that orders the production of antibodies.

ARTIFICIAL INSEMINATION. The placement of semen into a woman by means of a syringe.

AUTOGRAFT. Transplantation of tissue from one part of the body to another.

AUTONOMY. The principle that competent individuals have the right to make their own medical decisions.

BENEFICENCE. The principle that there is an obligation to help others.

BIOETHICS. The area of philosophy that concerns ethics as it applies to problems that arise from the biological sciences.

BIOMEDICINE. The practice of medicine with science as its foundation.

BRAIN DEATH. The permanent cessation of all brain functioning.

BRAIN STEM. The part of the brain that directs physiological functioning.

CHORIONIC VILLI ASSAY. A procedure by which fluid from the fetal tissue of the placenta is obtained for prenatal testing.

CHROMOSOME. A strand of DNA.

CLONING. Asexual reproduction producing an organism genetically identical to the one from which it derives.

COMA. A state of unconsciousness from which the patient cannot be aroused.

COMPETENCE. The ability to make rational decisions.

CONCEPTION. The fertilization of an ovum by a sperm.

CORTEX. That part of the brain responsible for thinking and feeling.

CYSTIC FIBROSIS. A heriditary disease characterized by the production of a gummy mucus that clogs the lungs.

CYTOSINE. One of the four nitrogenous bases that make up DNA.

DEOXYRIBONUCLEIC ACID. DNA, the chain of nitrogenous bases that order an organism's construction or functioning.

DIAGNOSIS. The determination of the nature of a diseased condition.

DIAGNOSTIC-RELATED GROUPS. DRGs, classifications of medical problems on which Medicare reimbursements are based.

DIALYSIS. See HEMODIALYSIS.

DNA. See DEOXYRIBONUCLEIC ACID.

DOWN'S SYNDROME. A condition caused by an extra chromosome 21 and characterized by mental retardation.

DRGS. See DIAGNOSTIC-RELATED GROUPS.

EMBRYO. A prenatal being from the time of implantation until about the eighth week after conception.

ETHICS. The principles from which moral rules are derived.

EUGENICS. The study of or the belief in the betterment of the human species through the control of mating, etc.

EUTHANASIA. As now understood, the intentional killing of a person who is near death in order to end severe pain, often referred to as "active euthanasia," to distinguish it from "passive," the termination of life-sustaining medical treatment.

FALLOPIAN TUBE. A tube through which the ovum moves from the ovary to the uterus; also the location where fertilization takes place.

FETUS. The prenatal being from about eight weeks after conception until birth.

GENE. A set of nitrogenous bases coding for the production of one protein.

GENOME. The entire set of genetic instructions for the construction and functioning of an organism.

GENOTYPE. The genetic makeup of an organism.

GERM CELL. A sex cell, either ovum or sperm.

GESTATION. The development in the womb, from implantation to birth.

GUANINE. One of the four nitrogenous bases that make up DNA.

HEMODIALYSIS. Mechanical intervention by which blood is cleansed of uric acid and urea.

HETEROGRAFT. Transplantation of tissue from a donor of another species.

HOMOGRAFT. Transplantation of tissue from a donor of the same species.

HUNTINGTON'S DISEASE. A hereditary disease characterized by deterioration of the brain and loss of voluntary muscular control, usually beginning in one's thirties.

IATROGENY. The causing of a medical disorder by medical treatment.

IMPLANTATION. The attachment of a preembryo into the wall of the uterus.

IN VITRO FERTILIZATION. Fertilization of an ovum outside the body.

INCOMPETENCE. The inability to function rationally.

INDICATION. A symptom that calls for a particular treatment.

INDUCED ABORTION. An abortion that is intentionally brought on.

INFANTICIDE. The killing of an infant.

INFERTILITY. A condition that makes fertilization and gestation difficult or impossible.

INFORMED CONSENT. Agreement to a medical treatment by a competent patient who understands the risks and benefits of the proposed treatment.

ISCHEMIA. The condition that results when the flow of oxygen-rich blood stops.

ISOGRAFT. Transplantation of tissue from a genetically identical donor.

JUSTICE. The principle of fairness, often stated in terms of the individual's being due what he or she deserves.

MEDICAID. A government program providing medical care to the poor.

MEDICALLY INDIGENT. Those people who cannot afford medical insurance but are ineligible for Medicaid.

MEDICARE. A government program providing medical care for the elderly.

MICROCEPHALY. Small head size, often associated with mental retardation.

MORALS. Personal rules about what actions are acceptable or unacceptable.

NONMALEFICENCE. The principle that one must do no harm.

OVUM. A female sex cell.

PALLIATION. The alleviation of pain.

PATERNALISM. The making of decisions for others.

PERSISTENT VEGETATIVE STATE. The condition that comes when the brain stem is functioning but the brain cortex is not.

PHENOTYPE. The genotype modified by the environment.

PHENYLKETONURIA. The inability to metabolize phenylalanine.

PKU. See PHENYLKETONURIA.

PREEMBRYO. A prenatal being from the time that cell division begins until implantation.

PROGNOSIS. A forecast of the effect of a disease or therapy.

PROTOCOL. The manner and timing of administering a drug, alone or in combination with other drugs, to maximize efficacy.

PVS. *See* PERSISTENT VEGETATIVE STATE.

QUICKENING. The time when a pregnant woman first feels prenatal movement by the unborn.

RESPIRATOR. *See* VENTILATOR.

SICKLE-CELL ANEMIA. A hereditary disease characterized by the inability of red blood cells to carry oxygen.

SOMATIC CELL. A body cell, as opposed to a sex cell.

SPERM. A male sex cell.

SPINA BIFIDA. A handicap that results from the failure of the neural tube to close.

SPONTANEOUS ABORTION. The natural ending of a pregnancy.

SUICIDE. The taking of one's own life.

SURROGACY. The gestation of a child that will be raised by others.

TAY-SACHS DISEASE. A genetic disease characterized by poor development and death by about the age of four.

TECHNOLOGICAL IMPERATIVE. The demand that every available technology be used to forestall death.

TECHNOLOGY. In medicine, the equipment, procedures, and drugs with which illness is treated.

TERATOGEN. An external agent that affects prenatal development.

THERAPEUTIC ABORTION. An abortion performed to protect the health or life of the mother.

THERAPEUTIC PRIVILEGE. Suspension of the obligation to tell the truth in cases where the truth might be damaging.

THYMINE. One of the four nitrogenous bases that make up DNA.

TRANSPLANT. The moving of tissue from one place to another.

TRIAGE. A procedure, first used with soldiers, by which treatment priorities are set based on the individual's medical condition and the resources at hand.

TRISOMY 21. The presence of a third chromosome 21, which causes Down's syndrome.

UTERUS. The organ in women in which gestation takes place.

VASECTOMY. The surgical procedure by which the vas deferens is cut to cause sterility in men.

VENTILATOR. A mechanical device that pumps air into the lungs.

VITALISM. The belief that everything should be done to save life.

ZYGOTE. The single cell produced by the fertilization of an ovum by a sperm.

SUGGESTED
READING

Bioethics is a very young field, so it is surprising that there is already a fine reference work. *The Encyclopedia of Bioethics,* edited by Warren T. Reich (New York: Free Press, 1978), is a good place to find basic information on bioethical issues. The *Hastings Center Report,* published six times a year, is an excellent journal that covers issues in every area of bioethics.

Written especially for young adults, *Thorny Issues: How Ethics and Morality Affect the Way We Live,* by John Langone (Boston: Little, Brown, 1981), takes up a wide variety of ethical questions, not just those that fall within the purview of bioethics. Another good book is *Bioethics: Dilemmas in Modern Medicine,* by Ann E. Weiss (Hillside, N.J.: Enslow Publishers, 1985).

Robert M. Veatch offers a thorough analysis of the Hippocratic code in *A Theory of Medical Ethics* (New York: Basic Books, 1981). In *Principles of Biomedical Ethics,* 3d edition (New York: Oxford University Press, 1989), Tom L. Beauchamp and James F. Childress offer a comprehensive explication of nonmaleficence, beneficence, autonomy, and justice. An excellent, very readable book is Ernlé W. D. Young's *Alpha and Omega: Ethics at the Frontiers of Life and Death* (Reading, Mass.: Addison-Wesley, 1989). Using cases, Young shows how ethical positions are developed. *How Brave a New World? Dilemmas in Bioethics,* by Richard A. McCormick, S.J. (Garden City, N.Y.: Doubleday, 1981), offers a thorough, well-written account of Roman Catholic thinking on a variety of issues.

B. D. Colen's *Hard Choices: Mixed Blessings of Modern Medical Technology* (New York: G. P. Putnam's Sons, 1986) explores ethical questions through extended interviews with everyday people who have had to grapple with very difficult medical situations. *Playing God: The New World of Medical Choices,* by Thomas and Celia Scully (New York: Simon and Schuster, 1987), is a good book for people who are trying to find their way through the health care system. The authors do not deal with the ethical dimensions of the decisions that must be made, but they offer a valuable listing of information sources for a variety of health problems.

A good—but much of it heavy going for the nonspecialist—book on issues stemming from genetic research is *Proceed with Caution: Predicting Genetic Risks in the Recombinant DNA Era,* by Neil A. Holtzman (Baltimore: Johns Hopkins University Press, 1989). More accessible are Robert Shapiro's *Human Blueprint: The Race to Unlock the Secrets of Our Genetic Script* (New York: St. Martin's Press, 1991) and Lois Wingerson's *Mapping Our Genes: The Genome Project and the Future of Medicine* (New York: E. P. Dutton, 1990). Daniel J. Kevles traces the history of the eugenics movement in his book *In the Name of Eugenics: Genetics and the Uses of Human Heredity* (New York: Alfred A. Knopf, 1985). In *Fabricated Man: The Ethics of Genetic Control* (New Haven: Yale University Press, 1970), Paul Ramsey considers the implications of genetic control, cloning, and the various reproductive technologies. An excellent overview of the new reproductive technologies is provided by "High-Tech Babies," one of the "Nova" series, first broadcast on 4 November 1986. For a small fee, a transcript can be obtained from WGBH Transcripts, 12 Western Avenue, Boston, Mass. 02134. Lori Andrews takes a comprehensive look at surrogacy in *Between Strangers: Surrogate Mothers, Expectant Fathers, and Brave New Babies* (New York: Harper and Row, 1989). *A Mother's Story: The Truth about the Baby M Case* (New York: St. Martin's Press, 1989), written with Loretta Schwartz-Nobel, is Mary Beth Whitehead's account of her disastrous experience with surrogacy. Gena Corea's *Mother Machine: Reproductive Technologies from Artificial Insemination to Artificial Wombs* (New York: Harper and Row, 1985) is a radical feminist critique of the field.

Ethical Issues in Death and Dying, edited by Robert F. Weir (New York: Columbia University Press, 1977), is a good collection of essays by professionals that range over problems at the end of life. On 13 December 1989, shortly after the U.S. Supreme Court heard oral arguments in the Nancy Cruzan case, the Public Broadcasting System aired a "Frontline" report describing the medical and legal particulars of the case, followed by a discussion of the ethical issues involved. A transcript of the program, "The Right to Die?" (show FLSP-1), can be obtained, for a small fee, from Journal Graphics, Inc., 267 Broadway, New York, N.Y. 10007. A moving account of one woman's struggle with amyotrophic lateral sclerosis—Lou Gehrig's disease—and her decision to die by voluntary euthanasia is provided by Andrew H. Malcolm in *This Far and No More* (New York: Times Books, 1987). Derek Humphry and Ann Wickett survey euthanasia in *The Right to Die: Understanding Euthanasia* (New York: Harper and Row, 1986). Readers should keep in mind that Humphrey and Wickett define euthanasia very loosely.

A first-rate book on neonatology is Robert F. Weir's *Selective Nontreatment of Handicapped Newborns: Moral Dilemmas in Neonatal Medicine* (New York: Oxford University Press, 1984). In *The Long Dying of Baby Andrew* (Boston: Little, Brown, 1983) Robert and Peggy Stinson provide an intimate diary chronicling their traumatic experience with one neonatal intensive care unit.

In *Ethics at the Edges of Life: Medical and Legal Intersections* (New Haven: Yale University Press, 1978), Paul Ramsey explores the reasoning behind court decisions concerning abortion and care at the start and at the end of life.

Daniel Callahan offers a provocative, fine analysis of how the process of aging has been changed by advances in medicine, how our view of aging has changed, and the implications for the allocation of scarce resources in *Setting Limits: Medical Goals in an Aging Society* (New York: Simon and Schuster, 1987). His most recent book, *What Kind of Life? The Limits of Medical Progress* (New York: Simon and Schuster, 1990), carries the arguments in *Setting Limits* further, proposing a complete rethinking of our notion of what is health and what is appropriate care.

A good place to begin when considering the issue of abortion is Lennart Nilsson's richly illustrated book *A Child Is Born* (New York: Delacorte Press, 1990). Now over twenty years old, Daniel Callahan's *Abortion: Law, Choice and Morality* (New York: Macmillan, 1970) remains an eminent text on the topic. In *Science and the Unborn: Choosing Human Futures* (New York: Basic Books, 1988), Clifford Grobstein analyzes the gestational period with a view to arriving at a status for the unborn. *New Perspectives on Human Abortion,* edited by Thomas W. Hilgers, Dennis J. Horan, and David Mall (Frederick, Md.: University Publications of America, 1981), is a collection of thirty-one essays supporting the pro-life position. Glanville Williams's *Sanctity of Life and the Criminal Law* (New

York: Alfred A. Knopf, 1974) looks at the meeting of law and morality. In *Abortion: The Clash of Absolutes* (New York: W. W. Norton, 1990), Laurence Tribe offers an analysis of abortion law, as well as a solid survey of the case for liberal abortion laws. Roger Rosenblatt explores why the issue of abortion has been more divisive in the United States than in any other society in *Life Itself: Abortion in the American Mind* (New York: Random House, 1992).

ACKNOWLEDGMENTS

This is a book only because of some people who gave unstintingly of themselves. The Reverend Ann S. Charles helped me get launched. Jonathan Lanman, as fascinated as I by bioethics, guided the project and edited the manuscript with great thoughtfulness. Terence Bailey, the copy editor, smoothed the text as he rooted out typos. Kathleen Nolan, M.D., vetted the manuscript with considerable care, for which I am very grateful. Any errors that remain, or that crept in, are all mine.

I am particularly indebted to the Hastings Center, in Briarcliff Manor, New York, which accepted me into its Visiting Scholar Program. For five weeks in the winter of 1990, I was free to drop in on the associates, roam the library, attend conferences, and eat my brown-bag lunch. I must explain that lunch at the Hastings Center is comprehensive nourishment. Lunch is the time when the entire staff—learned, seeking, empathic, witty—comes together for what invariably turns into a freewheeling foray into one or another area of bioethics. Always returning to first premises to genuinely think about them anew, everyone there wears his or her considerable professionalism lightly. The staff is remarkable for its openness and warmth. For me, the Hastings Center represents beneficence itself.

INDEX

Abortion, xii, 25–27, 31, 117–18, 121–138
  fetal indications for, 123–125
  maternal indications for, 121–122, 125
  parental consent and, 132–134
  strict laws on, 127–129, 138
  teenagers and, 133, 134
Active euthanasia, xii, 63–68
Adkins, Janet, 70–71
AIDS, 5–6, 19, 106, 116
Aiken, Henry David, 3–5
Alzheimer's disease, 70, 71
American Academy of Pediatrics, 82
American Hospital Association, 58
Amniocentesis, 124
Anscombe, G. E. M., 59
Aristotle, 13, 120
Artificial insemination, 33
  with donated sperm (AID), 39–40, 45, 46
Augustine, Saint, 69, 120
Autonomy, 15–18, 31, 60, 88, 113
Ayala family, 100–101

Baby Doe rules, 81–82, 85
Baby M, 41–43
Bauer, Emily, 47, 50–51, 67, 68
Beauchamp, Tom, 18, 66
Beneficence, 7–9, 11, 17, 52, 54, 62–64, 74, 75, 80
Blackmun, Harry, 130
Bopp, James, Jr., 60–61
Brain death, 50, 58–59
British Voluntary Euthanasia Society, 63
Broderick, John, 122
Brown, Louise, 35

Callahan, Daniel, 108–109, 111
Calvert, Crispina and Mark, 43–44
Carlson, Rick, 112
Carr, Pamela, 126
Catholics. See Roman Catholic Church
Chemotherapy, 8
Child Abuse Prevention and Treatment Act, 82
Children's Defense Fund, 116

Childress, James, 18, 66
Chorionic villi assay, 124
Christianity, 7, 69
Clark, Barney, 52
Cloning, 46
Columbia-Presbyterian Medical Center, 104
Congress, U.S., 24, 35, 96
Constitution, U.S., 57, 130, 131, 136
Corea, Gena, 32
Cowart, Dax, 53
Crick, Francis, 24
Cruzan, Nancy, 59–63, 89, 113
Cuomo, Mario, 137
Cystic fibrosis, 26, 123

Davis, Edwina, 126
Davis, Junior Lewis and Mary Sue, 37, 44
Deontological theories, 5
Diagnostic-related groups (DRGs), 107–108
Dialysis, 93–94, 96, 97
high cost of, 94, 103
DNA, 21–24, 28
Donaldson, Thomas, 19–20
Down's syndrome, 78–81, 85, 91, 124

Eugenics, 30
Euthanasia, 4, 63–68
Euthanasia Society of America, 63
Evans, J. Claude, 131

Fetal indications, abortions performed on, 123–125
Fieger, Geoffrey, 71
Final Exit (Humphry), 69
Finkbine, Sherri, 123, 124
FK-506, 98
Fletcher, Joseph, 20, 46, 91
Flowers, Robert C., 130
Food and Drug Administration (FDA), 123

Galton, Francis, 29
Gene therapy, xii, 23–25, 28–30, 32
Glazer, Shep, 96
God committees, 96
Gregg, Norman, 123
Gregory of Nyssa, Saint, 120

Handicapped children
care of, 79–80, 92
quality of life
considerations for, 89–90
Harvard Medical School Ad Hoc
Committee to Examine the Definition of Brain Death, 49–50
Hastings Center, 18
Health and Human Services, U.S.
Department of, 81, 82, 85, 116
Health care
high costs of, xii, 103–109, 113, 115–116
for terminally ill, 110
Health insurance, 103–104, 108
Hemlock Society, 71
Hennepin County Medical Center, 113
Hermann J. Muller Repository for
Germinal Choice, 30
Hippocratic Oath, 6–7, 127
HMOs (health maintenance organizations), 107
Hospices, 110
Houle, Lorraine and Robert, 83, 87
Howard, Coby, 114
Humphry, Derek, 69
Huntington's disease, 26, 27
Hyde, Henry, 125

Illinois Department of Children and
Family Services, 84
"Infant Doe," 81, 83
Infanticide, 76, 90–92
Informed consent, 17, 61, 65, 122
Insurance, health, 103–104, 108. See
also Medicaid; Medicare
International Kidney Exchange, 102

In vitro fertilization (IVF), 33–38, 43, 44

Jacobs, H. Barry, 102
Jehovah's Witnesses, 16
Jewish Chronic Disease Hospital, 15
Johns Hopkins Hospital, 79, 80, 89, 91
Johnson, Anna, 43–44
Justice, 12–14, 18, 94

Keane, Noel, 40
Kelsey, Frances, 123
Kennedy Institute of Ethics, 18
Kevorkian, Jack, 70–72
Killea, Lucy, 137
Klein, Martin and Nancy, 122
Koenig, Barbara, 54
Kolbert, Kathryn, 134
Krol, John Cardinal, 131

Latimer, Elizabeth, 68
Leukemia, 100, 101, 114
Living wills, 58, 60, 61
Locke, John, 12
Longmore, Paul, 111
Lorber, John, 77–78, 90

McAfee, Larry, 110–111
McCanse, Thad C., 62
McCorvey, Norma (Jane Roe), 129
McFall, Robert, 9–10
Maguire, Daniel, 67
Maher, Leo, 137
Malcolm, Andrew, 56–57, 64
Maternal health indications for abortions, 121–122
Maternal life indications for abortions, 121–122, 125
Medicaid, 12, 14, 101, 103, 105, 111, 115, 116, 132
Medicare, 103, 107, 111
Miscarriage, 123
Mueller, Pam and Robert, 84
Muller, Jessica, 54

National Institutes of Health, 24
National Right to Life Committee, 116
Nazis, 15, 64–66
Nelson, Lawrence, 82
Neonatology, 73–92
Nonmaleficence, 7, 8, 11, 52, 53, 63, 67, 87

Ordinary/extraordinary distinction, 51–54
Oregon Health Services Commission, 115–116
Organ donation, 99–102
Organ transplantation, xii, 47–48, 50, 97–103
  high cost of, 102–103, 114
  rejection of, 98

Palliation, 67, 68
Passive euthanasia, xii, 67
Peter Bent Brigham Hospital, 47
Phenylketonuria (PKU), 27
Planned Parenthood, 127
Planned Parenthood v. Casey, 134
Plato, 120
Potter, Ralph, 128
Prenatal testing, xii, 25–26
Pro-choice movement, 117–119, 126, 132, 133, 136, 138
Pro-life movement, 117–119, 125, 126, 131–133, 135, 138
Protestants, 45
Public Agenda Foundation, 115

Quality-of-life considerations, 53–54
  for handicapped children, 89–90
Quill, Timothy, 71–72
Quinlan, Karen Ann, 56–60, 89

Ramsey, Paul, 46, 53–54, 75
Raskind, Murray, 71
Reagan, Ronald, 81, 82, 106, 133–134
Rehabilitation Act (1973), 81, 82

Rhoden, Nancy, 86–87
Right-to-die cases, 56–63, 89, 113
Rios, Elsa and Mario, 37
Roberts, Barbara, 116
Roe v. Wade (1973), 129–135
Roman Catholic Church, 34–35, 45,
    51, 120, 121, 136, 137
Rothman, Barbara Katz, 44, 88
Rubella, 123, 128
Rust v. Sullivan (1991), 132
RU-486, 138

Saikewicz, Joseph, 8, 54
Schecter, Marshall, 41
Schmokel, Varian, 14
Scribner, Belding H., 97
Selective nontreatment of infants,
    87–88
Sex predetermination, 31–32
Shimp, David, 9–10
Short, John, 122
Sinsheimer, Robert, 21
Smith, Alyssa, 9, 10
Smith, David, 39, 70
Sorkow, Harvey, 41
Sperm banks, 38
Spina bifida, 77, 90, 123
Starzl, Thomas, 98
Stern, Elizabeth, 40–43, 45
Stern, William, 40, 41, 45
Stinson, Andrew, 75–76, 89
Stinson, Robert, 75–76
Suicide, 68–72
Supreme Court, U.S., 60, 62, 81,
    129, 130, 132–135
Surrogacy, 40–46
Szasz, Thomas, 70

Tay-Sachs disease, 25–26
Teen pregnancy, 5–6, 133
Teleological theories, 5
Teratogens, 123, 124
Thomas Aquinas, Saint, 51,
    120
Thalidomide, 123, 128
Tooley, Michael, 91–92
Transplants. See Organ
    transplantation
Triage, 94–95
Truman Medical Center, 133
Tuskegee Syphilis Study, 15

Ultrasound, 124
United Nations, 19
United Network for Organ Sharing,
    102

Ventilators, 48–50, 56, 111, 113

Wade, Henry, 129
Wanglie, Helga and Oliver, 113
Watson, James, 24
Webster v. Reproductive Health Ser-
    vices, Inc., 133, 134
Weddington, Sarah, 129, 130
Whitehead, Mary Beth, 40–45
Whitehead, Richard, 41
Williams, Glanville, 136
Willowbrook State School, 15
Wolf, Susan, 61, 113
World Health Organization, 19
World War I, 94
World War II, 10, 63, 95

Zachary, R. B., 78